CAMPUS ENGLISH

A Problem-solving Approach to Study Skills

David Forman, Frank Donoghue, Susan Abbey, Bryan Cruden and Ian Kidd (Project Co-ordinator)

A Centre for British Teachers Project

First published 1990
Revised Edition published 1991
Reprinted 1992, 1994

Published by MACMILLAN PUBLISHERS LTD
London and Basingstoke

ISBN 0 – 333 – 52234 – 6

Printed in Hong Kong

A CIP catalogue record for this book is available from the British Library

ACKNOWLEDGEMENTS

The authors and publishers would like to thank the following for permission to reproduce copyright material: The Daily Telegraph plc. for a news item by James O'Brien in the issue dated 27 October, 1987. (c) Daily Telegraph plc. 1990.
Penguin Books Ltd. for extracts from *Nuclear Power* by Walter C. Patterson (Second Edition, 1983).
The Press Association Ltd. for a news item reproduced in *The Independent*, 27 October, 1987.
Times Newspapers Ltd. for a news item by Michael Dynes in *The Times*, 27 October, 1987.

Cover photograph courtesy of
Sally and Richard Greenhill

CONTENTS

INTRODUCTION

A What is different about *Campus English*?

1 **A problem-solving approach** *Campus English* uses a task-based problem-solving approach. Students are expected to share their own knowledge and experience to find solutions to problems for which there may be no single correct answer.

2 **English for academic purposes** The students for whom this book has been designed are required to cope with demanding subject courses. However, most EAP coursebooks select texts which are far below the level which the students need for their studies. This book aims to bridge that gap in recognising students' language needs.

3 **Authentic texts and realistic tasks** *Campus English* contains authentic texts drawn from a variety of sources of the level and complexity students are likely to encounter in the course of their studies. The texts have been selected for their appropriateness to College or University level study and the tasks and activities have been carefully designed to build confidence and promote learning strategies. There is considerable emphasis on interaction to develop fluency through simulation, role plays, discussions and seminars in addition to study skills, such as: how to make notes from text; how to take notes from lecturers; how to extract main points, infer, and detect bias. Column 2 of the Skills Matrix in the Students' Book spells out these skills in more detail.

4 **International appeal** The material has been designed bearing in mind the needs of students in or from developing countries as well as from the developed world. The book does not assume a Western background but is truly international.

5 **English examination practice** The Teacher's Book in the Examination Edition contains a practice test of similar format to the British Council/University of Cambridge Local Examinations Syndicate International English Language Testing System (the IELTS test). This test is gaining increasing acceptance as a highly appropriate English Language qualification for English-medium study at tertiary level. The book offers practice in the skills needed for this test. The IELTS test is designed to test the English proficiency of students studying subjects other than English and the authentic texts employed in this book offer valuable practice in this. There is practice and preparation for all the components of the test including interview practice, listening tasks, multiple-choice exercises and study skills exercises. There is a test practice section at the end of each Unit in the Teacher's Book of both editions.

6 **Co-operative language learning** The book is based on the principle of co-operation rather than competition. Students are asked to co-operate with each other to arrive at an answer.

7 **An integrated skills approach** Each unit of this book is basically a collection of interlinked texts and tasks. The task types reflect the sort of activities students have to carry out as part of a course of study at college.

The choice of task type has been the result of a study of the needs of pre-university students.

One of the main principles here, as in subject study, is that tasks are not done in isolation, but follow on from and depend on each other. The advantage of this in an English course book is that work is motivating, realistic and dynamic.

B Who is *Campus English* for?

1 **Students** This book has been written for intermediate to advanced level students who are required to cope with demanding subject courses at tertiary (College or University) level at pre-tertiary level, and who need to improve their command of English for more effective study. *Campus* contains authentic texts of the level and complexity students are likely to encounter on Englishmedium courses during their first year of tertiary level study. The book is intended for students studying any Arts or Science subject and the different themes of each unit reflect this. Some units are oriented more towards the Arts than Science and vice versa but the material has been tested with both groups and it is the language skills which students learn and practise which are of paramount importance. Students will be improving their skills through stimulating material which may be outside their field of study and this may broaden their interests.

2 **Courses** This book may be used with students on courses varying in length from 3–4 weeks (*e.g.* pre-sessional courses) to a year's duration. The book could also form part of the resources for a course which may be longer than a year.

C The role of the teacher

1 **The student-centred approach** The book aims to be student-centred rather than teacher-centred. It is expected that the teacher's role will be that of monitor and facilitator rather than director. The aim is to promote learner independence from the teacher and students should be encouraged to work without intervention by the teacher. The teacher is not expected to know all the answers and in many cases there is no single 'right answer'. The teacher's task is to facilitate the process by which students arrive at an answer. Students may be encouraged to disagree in their answers, and what is important is how students justify their choice, rather than arriving at a correct answer. In this way, students will develop confidence in their own opinions. In further education, it is necessary to be prepared to question and not always expect tailor-made answers. One of the important overall objectives of the book is to train students in this. It is a major tactic that students should learn to employ for effective study. The focus of the activities in *Campus* is on interaction and discussion leading to the completion of the task, rather than on getting right answers.

2 **Groupwork** It may be helpful to organise the class in such a way that students can sit together in pairs or groups, enabling the teacher to move around the class monitoring groupwork. The teacher is not expected to sit or

stand at the front of the class all the time and students will often be required to work on their own, with a partner and in a group all in the same lesson. Discussion and interaction among students are all-important and arranging desks in groups rather than rows will help to promote this. If it is not possible to maintain a permanent group arrangement of desks as recommended, students can quickly become accustomed to moving into and out of groups with minimum disruption. With this group approach, it is not necessary to stream students, the success of the tasks is based on co-operation rather than competition.

3 **No subject knowledge required** Most of the teachers who use this book will be English teachers rather than subject specialists, and the book is designed with English teachers in mind. No specialist subject knowledge is required on the part of the teacher.

In deciding how to use this book with your students, it is more useful to ask: 'Will my students be able to complete this task successfully?' rather than: 'Will my students be able to understand this text?'

The level of the task is more important than the level of the text. All the necessary information for the student to complete the tasks successfully is contained in the book. There will be no need to refer to other sources, except in Section 5 of each unit (see **How the book is organised**). There is an extensive Answer Key.

To take an example of a task and the text with which it is used, look at this extract below, taken from Unit 6: A Brave New World.

Produced according to "state-of-the-art" technology and tested to the most stringent international quality control standards (including WHO guidelines), Engerix-B. shows an outstanding purity profile. It is highly immunogenic, i.e. confers a high degree of immunity, as demonstrated by the most sensitive *in vivo* and *in vitro* methods.

An intensive clinical investigation program was initiated in 1984. Today, more than 3000 vaccinees have been successfully enrolled into clinical trials carried out in European, African and Asian countries. These trials, supervised by leading authorities in the field of hepatitis B prevention, have confirmed the excellent clinical profile of the product. Reactions were rare, mild and transient in nature. The incidence of reactions was similar to that observed with plasma-derived vaccines and consisted mainly of local soreness and occasionally mild and transient systemic reactions (e.g. tiredness, headache, fever).

Seroconversion rates of close to 100% have been achieved.

This is taken from an advertisement for a medical product called Engerix-B. This text is clearly addressed to doctors, pharmacists and others in the medical profession. An English teacher would not be expected to explain such phrases as:

'*in vivo* and *in vitro* methods'
'plasma-derived vaccines'
'systemic reactions'
'seroconversion rates'

Technical vocabulary of this sort is no cause for alarm on the part of the teacher or students. Students should be able to identify the context of the text and should be encouraged to do so ('Who do you think this is written for/by?'). The actual vocabulary is only likely to be of relevance to students in the medical field, who can be encouraged to look it up in their subject textbooks or a medical dictionary.

Look now at the tasks which the students are asked to complete for this text:

D5 *a* The text is overwhelmingly in favour of this genetically engineered product. Pick out and note down phrases which display this.
Check your list with that of a partner.
Discuss the following questions with other members of your group.
b Who do you think this text was written for?
c Who do you think it was written by?
d What do you think is the purpose of the text?

The purpose of the task here is to enable students to identify language which is used to persuade, to identify the author's intention and the context of the text. The key symbol indicates that suggested answers are given in the back of the book.

An English teacher with little or no knowledge of the subject matter would have no difficulty in monitoring students in this task. The use of 'difficult' texts which the teacher may not be able to explain fully should not be seen as presenting any kind of a threat.

D How the book is organised

1 **Themes and functions** Each unit has been organised around a central theme and with a teaching focus on language functions as follows:

Unit	Theme	Function/Skills
1 Help yourself	Appropriate technology	Description of process
2 Arresting stuff	Law and order	Cause and effect
3 A question of power	Energy	Comparison and contrast
4 Ringing the changes	Ecology	Description of trends
5 Food for thought	Agriculture	Explanation
6 Brave new world	Genetic engineering	Discussion and argument
7 Your good health!	Health	Evaluation
8 What's it all for?	Education	Independent learning

The functional focus in each unit is relevant to all students, whether on Arts or Science courses. The themes in each unit reflect issues and raise questions of concern to educated thinking individuals. Students are given an opportunity to consider controversial ethical issues in fields of enquiry which have been chosen for their topicality, interest and the problems they pose for modern society. The language skills which students will use to explore these themes are skills they will need in their own studies and these skills are more important than the actual themes themselves. It is not essential that students will be following a course in, for example, agriculture or any other of the themes. The theme of each unit remains deliberately unstated in the Students' Book.

It is not the main aim of this book to provide information on, or teach about health programmes, technology or genetic engineering. These topics are used as vehicles for teaching skills.

While some topics are not directly relevant to everybody's area of study, they are accessible to students of all disciplines. The authors have been careful to choose topics of universal interest and to maintain a balance of scientific and arts materials.

2 **Organisation of units** Each unit is divided into five sections:

Section 1: An introduction to the theme, asking students to focus on the topic and problems related to it.

Section 2: The main teaching focus of the Unit where the functions and skills to be learnt and practised are introduced.

Section 3: Extension activities. Practice in the skills and functions of the Unit.

Section 4: Fluency activity. Putting the skills together by means of a simulation or role play, encouraging freer and more natural use of the language practised in the Unit. Students are required to find their own solution to a specific problem. Teachers should encourage fluency rather than accuracy in this section.

Section 5: A summary of the skills practised in the Unit and how these can be extended to the student's own subject area.

It is important that students see the relevance of what they are being asked to do in their own area of study and in this section they will be given an opportunity to relate what they have been doing to their subject area. The English teacher is not expected to be in a position to do the task for the students, but it is important that teachers check that the tasks are completed. Teachers may be tempted to omit this section if they cannot immediately see its purpose, but it is vital that students see that what they have been doing in the first four sections of the Unit has a bearing on their own studies. In this Section, students are encouraged to look outside this book. Arts students may find it helpful to look at one of their own subject textbooks in Section 5 of a Unit which may have had a 'Science flavour' (such as Unit 4: Ecology). Similarly, Science students may find it helpful to use a Science text for Section 5 in a unit such as Unit 2 (Law and Order).

E Vocabulary

One of the primary purposes of *Campus English* is for students to develop the ability to understand the gist of a text without necessarily understanding the meaning of every word. Students are not expected to look up every unfamiliar word and should be discouraged from doing so. They should be encouraged to assess the likely usefulness of the word to them and to use contextual clues to work out the meaning.

The many texts in each of *Campus English* are a rich resource for vocabulary work. Students' needs will vary according to the subject they are studying, their level of proficiency in English and their ability to learn. A Geography student, for example, would be more likely to need to know vocabulary from 'A question of power' (Unit 3) than 'Your good health!' (Unit 7). For these reasons, vocabulary exercises are given in the Teacher's Book rather than the Students'

Book. There are many different types of supplementary exercise focussing on the vocabulary from the texts in each unit, with further suggestions which teachers may like to follow up on their own. Teachers should feel free to use these exercises according to the needs of their students. There are suggestions for starting and maintaining a vocabulary system in the Students' Book, guidance on identifying vocabulary problems and strategies for working out the meaning from context.

F Using the book

Campus English is not a workbook. 'Workbook activities' where students are required to write in the book itself have been deliberately avoided, enabling the book to be used with more than one group at a time without the distraction of another student's pencilled notes.

1 **A course book** This book can be used as a course book and worked through from cover to cover. If handled in this way, it guarantees a steady build-up of skills.

The book is structured in such a way that skills are always taught before they are practised. All skills are then recycled in later units.

In addition, the more basic skills and functions are introduced early on in the book, while the more complicated ones come later.

The later units are also less guided in that they allow students more autonomy in how they organise their work, and more choice in selecting activities and tasks.

It will be evident to teachers that each unit incorporates a lot of practice material. Once teachers feel that the students have sufficient command of language or skills, they may elect to omit parts or indeed whole sections of units and move more quickly on to the freer practice sections of each unit, (Sections 4 and 5).

2 **Source material** On the other hand, teachers may prefer to be more flexible in their use of the book and treat it as source material or select skills for development according to the particular needs of their students. Teachers will be able to choose relevant tasks as they feel necessary using the Skills Matrix at the front of the Students' Book. It is not essential to work through the book from beginning to end. This will pose no problem since the material is not graded in difficulty from Unit 1 to Unit 8. The reason for this is that realistic listening and reading texts are used throughout and therefore the text difficulty level is constant. Task difficulty level is graded within each unit, but not within the book.

G Evaluation

1 **Written work** In evaluating students' written work, teachers are advised to concentrate on one or two of the more serious errors their students make rather than marking all faults at once. A page full of red ink does little to help student motivation. Teachers should look for appropriate criteria. For example, in describing a process it would be helpful to examine the use of the passive and tenses. Tell students in advance what to watch out for. Vary the skills you mark for. The teachers' tips offer advice on appropriate skills to look for.

An appropriate strategy for the teacher would be:

a Decide the marking criteria in advance.
b Tell your students what to watch out for.
c Students complete writing task.
d Mark according to the criteria.
e Provide feedback and explanation.

It is important for students to realise the kind of mistakes they make and to develop strategies to correct them.

2 **Oral work** A great deal of the oral work in this book aims to develop fluency, and it is important that teachers do not interrupt the flow by correcting students' mistakes. This does not mean abdicating responsibility for corrections but monitoring recurrent mistakes which can be discussed with the class, group or individual. In Section 4 of each Unit, make a note of mistakes as they arise and provide feedback later. Keeping a note of common mistakes also enables the teacher to determine the needs of the class and decide on priorities.

H The background to this book

Campus English is the result of a Study Skills in English Materials Writing Project for university and pre-university students studying Arts or Science subjects. The authors have been working with the Centre for British Teachers in Malaysia, preparing students for 'A' Level, the British Council/University of Cambridge Local Examination Syndicate International English Language Testing System (the former ELTS test) and for university level study in English.

It was the lack of a good EAP source book for these students which led eventually to the writing project which produced this book. Each unit and the practice test were trialled with a target group in Malaysia before publication. This trialling exercise provided extensive feedback from teachers and students and the material has been significantly modified as a result.

STARTING ON CAMPUS ENGLISH

Teacher's notes

Students' Book Pages xiv–xvii.
This short introduction explains to students what the book is about and how to use it. However, it isn't just an explanation but contains tasks for the students to work through.

A1 The book does not aim to help students with *c* or *e*. The other statements are true.

Teachers should not discuss this task until after the students have checked their answers in **A2**.

B1 Students are encouraged here to note where their own language weaknesses lie and to find out where these skills are covered in the book. Students should recognise the distinction between skills which are taught and those which are practised.

B2 The aim here is for students to use the section headings within each unit as a clue to where the topics are covered. The titles of the units themselves do not always provide the answer.

Issues mentioned in Paragraph 4	Unit	Clue
Whether man has the right to create animals	4	Tampering with life
The best type of education system	8	The world of education
Improving agricultural output	5	Food for thought
The causes and effects of crime	2	All headings

B3 The aim of this exercise is for students to justify their choice. When the pairs compare answers, they should find that there are some cases where they disagree. Teachers should ask students their reasons for making their choice.

Possible answers are:
a C or D
b B (C and D are possible)
c D (B possible)
d B (C possible)

C **Book Talk** The aim here is for the class to compare *Campus English* with another ELT book for students of a similar level and decide which they would recommend. Students are introduced to the idea of group work and exchanging ideas in a meeting.

C1 **Preparation** Teachers may like to bring in several copies of different texts which are suitable for comparison at the start of this lesson. It is suggested that students be allowed an hour to prepare their case, more if they need it.

The role of Chairperson should be taken by a student.

For the group preparation teachers should ensure there is appropriate division of labour to ensure that each student is occupied, *e.g.* as secretary, spokesperson, book critic.

Students should be encouraged to analyse strengths and weaknesses in the book they are examining.

Presentation Students should be discouraged from reading from prepared papers (though they may like to use notes) and it should be stressed that this is a meeting rather than a debate, so there should be opportunities for discussion.

During the presentation students should not be corrected. Teachers may like to note language weaknesses in oral presentations to give to individuals after this activity.

Teachers need not be concerned if the meeting is lively with strong opinions expressed; the aim of this activity is to promote fluency. A weak chairperson may need some assistance to ensure that the meeting arrives at a decision. Time limits for each group may help to keep things moving.

C2 **Evaluation** This should take the form of a class discussion. The aim here is for students to justify their views.

UNIT 1 · *Help yourself*

INTRODUCTION

As an early unit in this book, 'Help yourself' has the task of familiarising the students with the activity types that are to follow throughout.

Here students are encouraged to discuss among themselves in pairs or groups, to pool their ideas and language knowledge, to read and interpret texts quickly, to make notes in an appropriate and effective way and to use these notes as a basis for further work.

Some of these techniques may be new to students and therefore they will probably need encouragement. The objective is to establish the basis for co-operative learning, which will be maintained throughout the book.

Each student brings to the classroom a store of personal knowledge and experience. The aim is to capitalise on this and exploit it. In this Unit students will think about and discuss their experiences of technology, and what appropriate technology means to them.

OBJECTIVES OF THIS UNIT

Here we are mainly concerned with:

1 Teaching students to understand and interpret texts which describe processes.

2 Teaching students to use various forms of notes in order to summarise information in a concise and meaningful way.

Throughout the Unit a number of other study and exam skills are taught and practised. These are listed below section by section.

SECTION 1 – *SUMMARY*

In this section students will:

- learn to predict text content from excerpts.
- learn to work out the definition of a concept from examples.

Teaching tips

Page 1

A Start off by asking students

- what is meant by the term revolution?
- which piece of technology seems more modern?
- which do you think was most effective?

In fact both of these could be regarded as equally modern and equally effective if they solved the current needs of their society.

Page 1

A1 Suggested answers:

- Both fulfil a need in their society.
- They imply a large gap between the wealth and expectations of one society and another.
- To indicate a sudden and far-reaching change in the lives of the two societies.
- Although he doesn't state his preference, the writer describes the second revolution more sympathetically. If the students cannot see where the writer's sympathies lie, write the following key points from the first example on the blackboard.

200 minutes 100 people sonic boom $40,000,000

Ask the students to find the corresponding points in the second example. These are: 14 hours; a village; no sonic boom; $42.

Page 2

A2 *a* E.F. Schumacher was an economist, living in England, who pioneered the idea of intermediate (or appropriate) technology in the 1960's.

Before asking the students to read the text, you might discuss with them what they understand by the terms 'small is beautiful' and 'big is best'.

Supplementary exercise

You can give the students more practice in the skill of predictive reading by:

- distributing the first part of a text to the students.
- asking them to read it and predict what will follow.
- distributing the remaining part of the text and allowing the students to see if their predictions were correct.

Students can also practise this skill by themselves by pausing from time to time in their reading and trying to predict what will occur next.

Page 2

A2 *b* Example rewrite:

Developed countries should not give aid in the form of machinery as this does little to encourage self-sufficiency and independence. These goals can be achieved if instead they provide education and teach practical skills.

A2 *b* Supplementary exercise

If the students have difficulty performing this task an examination of the vocabulary may assist them.

This exercise will help students see the connections of key words in the text and thus should guide them towards a definition of Appropriate Technology.

Ask students to look at the three boxed texts on page 2.
Indicate to students that two important concepts in the text are the aid that is provided by the West and the idea of developing countries operating in an independent fashion.
Put these jumbled words and phrases on the blackboard and ask the students to organise them under the two headings, **Aid** and **Independence**.

give a man   local needs   self-supporting
supply him   cost   Western technology   imported
appropriate technology   help himself   teach a man
local purses   independence   dependent upon
helping him   make his own   self-reliant
fewer jobs locally   fitted local conditions.

Encourage students to refer to the use of these words in the text in order to decide if they are concerned with **Aid** and **Independence**.

Page 2

A2 *c* Suggested answers:

- Influenced by Schumacher: aid organisation, development planners, agriculturists, engineers, technologists.
- Changes: from 'physical' aid (skills, training); and an increased emphasis on aid for self-sufficiency and independence.
- Connection (1): less glamorous, 'smaller' beginnings can have more satisfactory results.
- Connection (2): small, cheap but reliable aid, skills-based.

Page 2

A3 *a* This statement introduces the ideas of economy (cheapness), maintaining job-availability and appropriacy to actual needs and conditions. It therefore reflects Schumacher's theme.

b Example definition:
Appropriate Technology is an approach to aiding developing countries which takes into consideration their needs, local conditions and the economic situation and which aims to help those countries to help themselves.

Giving definitions: Supplementary exercises

1 A definition is usually made up of three parts:
a The concept, item or thing to be defined.
b The group or class it belongs to.
c The characteristics it possesses.

2 When defining characteristics it is common to use *who* for a person and *which* for an object, animal or process but *that* can be used in place of either *who* or *which*. In certain cases *with* can be used to describe numerical characteristics such as speed and height.

concept/item to be defined	group/class	characteristics
A professional footballer	(is a person)	(who makes a living from playing football)
A durian	(is a fruit)	(which has a strong smell)

Exercise 1

The information in the 'group' and 'characteristics' columns is mixed up. Put the information into the correct order and then write a definition for each item.

Item	Group/Class	Characteristics
Elements	force	measuring atmospheric pressure
Gales	instruments	cannot be broken down into anything simpler by chemical means
Gravity	substances	(1) listening to the beating of the heart (2) listening to the sound of breathing
A catalyst	instruments	attracts objects to the centre of the earth
Barometers	organism	an average force of more than 62 km/h
A stethoscope	chemical substances	(1) lives on/in other animals (2) gets its food from other animals
A parasite	winds	accelerates a chemical reaction

Exercise 2

Draw another table like the one above and then complete it for the following items:

1 tractor
2 hoe
3 settlement
4 machine
5 squatter

SECTION 2 – *SUMMARY*

In this section students will:

– practise scanning a text to find particular information.
– learn to write notes on a process in flow chart form.
– learn to apply flow chart note-taking techniques to listening.
– learn to identify language which shows the sequence of events in a process.
– learn to recognise the coherent nature of a text by:
  a understanding the function of reference words.
  b recognising the use of equivalents.
– practise writing a short description.
– practise writing a coherent passage based on flow chart notes.
– practise giving a short talk to a group.

Teaching tips

Page 2

A1 Students may assume wrongly that only one process is being described here. This article in fact contains descriptions of three distinct processes, only one of which was successful. The successful attempt is described in the last three paragraphs of the article.

Problems faced by the villages:

– little money
– very hard work
– they had to pay for milling services 10 miles away.

Various kinds of help offered (3 kinds):

– a tractor
– a simple bicycle grinder
– the village smith was trained to make better tools.

Page 3

A2 A flow chart does require a litte more work to produce than a simple list. In order to persuade the students of the usefulness of flow charts as visual presentations, get them to do this brief exercise.

Divide the class into two groups. One group studies the list for 10 seconds while the other studies the flow chart for 10 seconds. After 10 seconds, tell the students to cover their books. Now ask them to rewrite the steps involved in the 'tractor donation section'. Give them **one minute** to do this. Finally, ask representatives from each group to read out their results. It is likely the 'flow chart' group will demonstrate better recall of the steps.

(You might care to use other examples of sequence/process lists and flow charts of your own, or perhaps from the students' subject textbooks, to repeat this exercise.)

Page 4

A3 It is more common to use a flow chart in the course of writing up notes, for example, after a lecture. However, flow charts can be used to take notes during a lecture when the sequence being described is a simple one. For exercise **A3**, suggest to the students that they note the steps in the listening extracts with a sufficient gap between each point and only 'box in' the information when they are sure a particular point has been completed. They should **not** draw the box first, before hearing and noting the information.

In addition, you might point out to the students:

- that their flow charts should always contain only key information.
- that this information should be abbreviated as much as possible.
- that each box should contain a complete step.
- that each step should be of roughly equal importance.
- that each box should be closed only when the step has been completed.

Page 4

A3 *a* and *b*

The tapescripts show, *in italics*, the steps in each process and in bold, the sequence markers.

It will probably be desirable to have the students listen again to the tape. Alternatively, you might find it more useful to read out the extracts to the class so that you can emphasise the steps and the sequence-markers.

Page 4

B1 Supplementary exercise

To enable the students to assess the writer's objective, ask them to read the text again and answer the following question. In this passage the writer's intention is to:

A advocate solutions to the world's housing problem.
B objectively describe the world's housing problem.
C critically evaluate the world's housing problem.
D draw attention to the world's housing problem.

The correct answer is *D*. The writer is concerned about the problem and wishes to share his or her concern with the reader. To do this makes extensive use of words and phrases which describe poor housing conditions.

Ask the students to list as many of these words and phrases as they can.

Their list should include most of the following:

homeless	no shelter
extremely poor housing	sleep in the steets
unhealthy environment	slums and squatter settlements

The effect of these words is to give a negative impression of the world's housing problem.

Ask the students to think of words which would provide a positive impression of a successful attempt to solve a housing problem.

It is unlikely that students will produce satisfactory alternatives which accurately convey the slight but significant changes in meaning. They may make excessive use of antonyms which provide too great a contrast.

For instance, an unhealthy environment and extremely poor housing will not be transformed into luxury housing overnight.

If the students did have such problems ask them to match the more positive sounding descriptions with the more negative ones they identified in the text.

low income housing area	sufficient shelter
adequate housing	healthier environment
housed	have access to simple shelter

A number of combinations are possible but the suggested equivalents are:

homeless = housed
extremely poor housing = adequate housing
unhealthy environment = healthier environment
no shelter = sufficient shelter
sleep in the streets = have access to sufficient shelter
slums and squatter settlements = low income housing areas

Page 5

B2 *b* This might be a good point to remind your students about appropriate use of tenses. If the person they choose to write about is dead, the dominant tenses will be the simple past and the past perfect. If the person is still alive, the tenses will be more mixed: the simple past will be used to describe completed actions, the present perfect for actions which began in the past and continue to the present (using expressions like *for* and *since*) and the simple present to describe facts about his or her present status.

B2 *c* You might wish to consolidate this work on referencing by writing on the blackboard selections from two or three of the students' paragraphs. You could then ask the class to suggest ways in which the individual student's work could be improved.

Page 6

C1 Academics sometimes use informal English words and phrases in their writing or during their lectures. This can confuse non-native speakers. However, it is sometimes possible for students to work out the meaning from context. Ask your students to guess the likely meanings of 'off the ground' and 'for peanuts' (= *started* and *very cheaply*).

Page 6

C1 *a* Point out to the students that they are asked to describe 'how the machine works', not what the operator does. They should consider therefore the workings of the device, *i.e.* the relationship between the wire mesh, tyre and crank, and the physical nature of the device, *e.g.* why a rubber tyre is used instead of a wooden or stone wheel.

c Suggested answer:
The pods are fed into the hopper at the rear of the machine. The crank handle is then turned, causing the tyre to revolve. The tyre rubs against the pods which have come down the chute and this causes the shells to

break. The groundnuts themselves are left unharmed and fall through the wire mesh. They are then collected in baskets below the machine.

Students often find difficulty in mastering the appropriate use of the passive. This might be a good moment to look at the different situations which govern the choice of active or passive or even imperative use of verbs.

Active Ask the students to describe what the operator of the peanut sheller does. They should use the active form of the appropriate verbs.

Example: The operator *puts* the peanuts in the hopper and places an empty basket at the bottom of the chute. He then *turns* the crank handle. He finally *removes* the basket of shelled nuts.

Point out to the students the form of the verbs.

Passive Ask students to look at the suggested answer above. Note that both active and passive uses occur.

The passive is normally used when describing processes or experiments. This is because it describes a state of affairs which is observable whoever the agent may be.

A rough generalisation for the use of active and passive is as follows:

1 Where the agent is known but irrelevant, use the passive.

In this suggested answer, 'The pods are fed into the hopper' – the agent who feeds in the pods is irrelevant.

2 Where the agent is known and relevant use the active.

In this suggested answer, 'The tyre rubs against the pods.' The crank handle, a part of the process, causes the tyre to do this.

In chemistry experiments, the verb 'react' is always active for this reason – it describes what happens between two or more known relevant agents.

Imperative Students often wrongly employ the imperative form of the verb when writing descriptions of process. In fact, this form should only be used when directions for use are being given. In this context, 'Place some peanuts in the hopper and a basket at the bottom. Then turn the handle' would be an adequate set of directions for use.
In a more general context suggest that the students look for as many examples of 'directions' as they can. They will find these in technical manuals (bicycle repair guides, *etc.*), recipe books, on aerosol shaving-foam cans, instant soup packets and so on.

The important general distinction students must make is that:

– the active describes who does what.
– the passive describes what happens.
– the imperative tells you what to do.

Page 6

C2 *a* Here students have to develop solutions to problems. When they have formed into groups, make sure that each of the four problems is being dealt with. Remember it is the student's ability to order an explanation into a series of steps which is important in this exercise, **not** the feasibility of the solutions themselves.

Page 7

C2 *b* While the blackboard presentations are being made, it might be a good idea to move around the class to ensure that the students are attempting the note-making task.

c The students should evaluate each other's flow charts according to the criteria given on Page 15 of this book.

SECTION 3 – *SUMMARY*

In this section students will:

- learn to predict the content of a text by using clues in the title, introduction and accompanying illustrations.
- learn to skim a text to pick out the main points and the overall aim.
- practise scanning a text to find relevant information.
- practise comparing a number of texts on a similar topic.
- learn to summarise information from different sources in table form.
- practice taking notes while listening.
- practise writing a short description of two contrasting problems.

Teaching tips

Page 7

A1 *a* At this stage you should not be too concerned with the 'correctness' of the students' responses. It is important that they develop the ability to predict content by **practising** the techniques described in this section.

b It should be stressed to the students that skim-reading is a very important skill. It can save valuable time and makes it easier to decide quickly on the relevance of material to their studies.

They should be encouraged to practise skimming in their own reading.

You should perhaps point out that in various tests of English – notably the IELTS Test – the student's ability to deal with a large amount of text in a very short time is actively tested. In this sort of activity, the 'quick-reading' skills of skimming and scanning (discussed below – Section 3 **A4** on page 20 of the Teacher's Guide) are of vital importance.

In this exercise and in other similar ones that you may give the students, it would be a good idea to impose a time limit on their skimming or scanning.

In this case it is recommended that you give the students about **one minute** for the skim-reading.

Page 9

A2 The steps describing the process are identifiable but they are sometimes disguised by the descriptive style of the writer. This contrasts with the more straight-forward style of the writer of 'Right Machine for the Job'.

A3 *a* It is unlikely that students will feel a flow chart is suitable here as this passage does not describe a process.

Page 9

A3 *b* A suggested alternative is to draw up a table like the one below:

OPP	UN
Small-scale body	International Dev. Agency
Trial and error approach	Target-oriented aims
Costs reduced	High cost
Local involvement	Centralized management

c OPP involved the people in active decision-making and participation. It acknowledged the financial position of the people. The UN project did neither.

Pages 8–9

Supplementary exercise: A wise head

To help students to get an overall impression of an article it can be useful to focus their attention on the connotations of the vocabulary it contains.

The exercise that follows requires us to decide whether the vocabulary bears negative or positive connotations, and where these occur. This can help to identify the attitude of the writer to the subject.

Write up this selection of 10 words from the test in a random order:

confidence festering sopport inadequate ineffective
risks too costly cost-efficient improve philanthropic

Ask students to divide these words up into two classes. Don't suggest what the titles are at this stage – but have the students make these suggestions.

Students should be told to examine these words in their context, in order to understand their meaning. If necessary, students should check the words in a dictionary.

Discuss the different ways of dividing up the words that students suggest.

If the class hasn't yet thought of it, suggest dividing the selection of words according to whether they have a **positive** or **negative** sense.

Students should suggest the following two lists:

Positive	**Negative**
support	festering
confidence	risks
philanthropic	too costly
improve	ineffective
cost-efficient	inadequate

Ask students to extend their lists by scanning the text for more positive/negative vocabulary.

Ask the students if the text has a more positive or more negative 'slant'.

If students were to actually count the words and compare the numbers with positive and negative connotations, there would not be a great difference between the two.

However, if the teacher asks students to look in particular at the last paragraph, they will discover an overwhelming number of positive phrases. This suggests that the writer wishes to leave the reader with a strong positive impression of this project.

The teacher who wishes to exploit this text further could direct the students' attention to the positive phrases mentioned above. Suggest that the students quickly note down as many examples of positive phrases as they can from the last two paragraphs of the passage.

The students should identify the following phrases:

- within the reach of the poorest
- substantial decrease in costs
- eliminating cutbacks
- drastic reduction (in costs)
- improving design of manholes, septic tanks
- project workers are inundated with requests
- individuals often get on with the work themselves

Although the writer of the article wishes to end this on a positive note which will reflect the success of the project, it is interesting to note that in all but one of the phrases above we find potentially **negative** vocabulary.

Ask the students to identify these negative possibilities. They are:

poorest
decrease
cutbacks
drastic
septic
inundated

Point out to students that these words assume a positive character only because of **context**, the words with which they are associated in the text.

Finally, ask the students to write sentences to show these six words performing a **negative** function.

It is to be impressed upon students that skimming and scanning techniques, in which single-word identification is an important guide to the likely content or viewpoint of a text, must be treated as investigative steps only and cannot form a definitive basis for deciding that the text contains information you want. Skimming or scanning must always be followed by a more intensive examination of the content.

Page 10

A4 *c* Scanning is another skill vital to the improvement of reading efficiency. Having decided that a text is likely to be useful in a general sense, the student may then want to locate and extract specific information.

Scanning involves finding that information as quickly as possible, without understanding the overall meaning of the rest of the text. For example, when the student is looking for his own name on a list of examination results, he **scans** the list. When he is looking for his favourite football team's results in the newspapers he **scans** the page.

'Sites and services scheme' is not itself a planning organisation; it is a **project** funded by the World Bank. However, if students have included it, this can be seen in a positive light. Gaining more information than is strictly relevant from scanning is preferable to inadequate scanning.

Page 10

A4 *e* Students may mention many differences in detail but should appreciate the fact that the OPP and Madras projects were successful because they took into account the needs and opinions of the people whereas the UN and Bombay projects were less successful because they were centrally planned and imposed without consultation.

Page 11

B Students should produce a table like this:

	African Village	Groundnuts	Orangi OPP	Orangi UN	Bombay	Madras
Scale	local/ small scale	small scale	local/ large scale	local/ large scale	local/large scale	local/large scale
Type of Problem	lack of good tools	inefficient and high-cost processing	lack of sewage facilities	lack of sewage facilities	insufficient and inadequate housing	insufficient and inadequate housing
Approach	discussion consensus self-help	devised in response to local needs	discussion consensus self-help	imposed	imposed	applied after consultation with the people

Page 11

C2 In this writing exercise, the students will have to make full use of various notes they have taken in the course of reading the passages throughout this Unit. Those who elect to write about the Thai groundnut sheller should refer to the description of the problem that machine was developed to counter.

You should pay particular attention to the students' use of appropriate tenses, use of active/passive voice and their ability to describe the **processes** of remedial action, ensuring that steps involved are clearly shown. Look out also for the students' use of reference words.

SECTION 4 – *SUMMARY*

In this section students will be engaged in:

- interpreting flow chart information.
- using available information to prepare a proposal.
- presenting a proposal in a persuasive way.
- looking critically at different solutions to a problem and challenging when necessary.

Teaching tips

Students may tend to believe that there is only one winning option. Before beginning the activity reassure them that it is possible for any of the villages to win. Everything depends on how effectively the case is put forward.

The representatives of the villagers can build on the information contained in the briefs but they should never try to contradict the basic facts it contains. Similarly, the state government should be aware that they cannot make a completely free choice. They have to work within the policy constraints mentioned in their brief.

When introducing the subject point out to the students that the three newspaper articles provide valuable background information. Students should read them to help strengthen their own case and be aware of the kind of arguments the other villagers may use.

The role of the teacher during these simulations should be that of observer rather than participant.

Try to encourage the students not to ask questions about grammar and do not correct their English. However, it is a good idea to note down any high frequency errors and use them as the basis for a future lesson that focuses on grammar and structures.

SECTION 5 – *SUMMARY*

Section 5 is in many ways the most valuable part of the Unit. There is, however, a danger that students may tend to ignore it if you do not draw their attention to its contents.

The most important thing to stress is that students should not be deceived into thinking that the flow chart is more important than the information it contains. Try to ensure that the students continue to practise these skills on a regular basis. One idea is to introduce a 'study skills session', where students use their newly acquired techniques to revise work under the supervision of a teacher. When they have acquired this habit of applying the skills they have learnt they should then be able to work on their own.

TEST PRACTICE

The following questions have been provided on the work in this Unit. Students will need a multiple-choice answer sheet.

READING The following questions test your ability to read and understand English.

Section 1

For each question, choose the sentence which is closest in meaning to the first sentence.

1 The fishermen's case was more urgent than the others.
  A The fishermen's case was not the most urgent.
  B The other cases were more urgent than the fishermen's.
  C The other cases were less urgent than theirs.
  D The other cases were as urgent as theirs.

2 We'll re-apply for extra funds as soon as possible.
A It's possible we'll re-apply for extra funds.
B We may well get extra funds soon.
C We will find extra revenue soon.
D We will apply again for more money immediately.

3 I think it was just about the right decision.
A I was right about the decision.
B I feel the decision was more or less fair.
C I think it was clearly the best decision.
D I believe it was the only possible just decision.

4 If their case hadn't been so strong, we wouldn't have lost.
A If our case had been stronger than theirs, they wouldn't have won.
B If it were not for the strength of their case, we would win.
C We would have lost if their case had been stronger.
D We wouldn't have lost if their case had been stronger.

5 The amount of money is higher than I expected.
A I expected there to be more money.
B I expected the amount of money to be higher.
C The money amounts to more than I expected.
D The money does not amount to as much as I expected.

6 I never dreamt I would ever live in a place like this.
A This is not the sort of place I would dream of living in.
B I dreamt I lived in a different kind of place.
C I expected I would live in a place like this.
D This is not the sort of place I expected I would live in.

7 The size and scale of this operation has never been undertaken before.
A The operation is not as large as some earlier operations.
B The operation of this undertaking depends on its size and scale.
C The operation is bigger than any previously attempted.
D Before undertaking this operation the size and scale had not been considered.

8 He believes firmly in establishing self-help programmes.
A His firm belief is that established self-help programmes deserve more help.
B He works for a firm which believes in helping itself to established programmes.
C He is committed to the idea of individuals solving their own problems.
D He wants very much to help establish programmes.

9 The health budget can only stretch so far.
A This is the point beyond which the health budget cannot go.
B There are limitations to what the health budget can pay for.
C So far the amount of money allocated to health expenses has been flexible.
D Only the expenditure on health is expected to increase very much.

10 Mr. Phan went on to outline the proposals.
A The suggestions were discussed in full.

B Mr. Phan spoke at tedious length about the proposals.
C A full explanation of the plans were given by Mr. Phan.
D The general content of the plans was described.

11 I think we've been overlooked.
A I've looked over what we believe.
B We haven't been given a chance to look.
C Our case has been looked into too much.
D Our case has been put to one side.

Section 2

... But the story is not one of unconditional success. For Orangi was divided into **1** sectors when the project started, with the DPP having responsibility for one and a UN community development programme the other. And sadly, the two programmes were **2** to co-operate. **3** is perhaps a classic example of the divergence of approach **4** international development agencies, geared to target-oriented aims, and small-scale bodies which tend to involve the people and work through **5** and error.

Arif Hasan, OPP's architect and consultant, confirmed the division and said that neither group could agree **6** work methods. The Bank **7** a sector of Orangi to the UN agency and set **8** the project for them. But it has now been wound up after $625,000 had been **9** on developing 35 lanes **10** three years, he explained.

Dr. Khan and his team have fulfilled their aim to reduce costs, and involve home owners in managing and paying for sanitary latrines in their homes and underground sewerage in their lanes.

A	B	C	D	
various	two	several	all three	**1**
willing	able	disinterested	unable	**2**
That	It	The programme	Co-operation	**3**
between	amongst	throughout	beside	**4**
trialling	experiment	trial	trying	**5**
with	to	for	on	**6**
awarded	allocated	loaned	showed	**7**
up	...	off	aside	**8**
invested	allocated	spent	embezzled	**9**
since	by	before	in	**10**

Section 3

To answer the following questions, read the newspaper articles in Section 4 on pages 14 to 15.

Questions on Article A

1 AT Phan
A is contemplating resignation as leader of the Fisheries Union.

B will definitely be a candidate in next month's elections.
C is a critic of the government's trade policy.
D is critical of the government's allocation of resources.

2 He believes Hamton's claim is justified by
A the lack of employment opportunities in Hamton.
B the absence of a natural harbour in Hamton.
C the need to develop processing and canning in the region.
D the amount of funds previously granted to the others.

3 To ensure its long term survival the region's fishing industry requires
A more natural harbours.
B increased investment in canning facilities.
C improved safety conditions on the boats.
D men prepared to stay on the boats.

4 AT Phan is demanding
A ultra modern plants.
B a natural harbour.
C a safe harbour.
D plants with primary facilities.

Questions on Article B

5 The opposition claims that the government
A is reducing the standard of living in rural areas.
B is not stopping a migration of capital to the towns.
C is failing to control the capitals standard of living.
D is no longer strongly pursuing its policies.

6 The main objective of the RPP is to
A introduce help to needy areas.
B bring about an overall increase in living standards.
C keep a tight control on government expenditure.
D improve the nation's trade figures.

7 The government claims the hospital in the capital
A needs funds to develop its infrastructure.
B has the infrastructure to develop doctors.
C has an infrastructure that needs more trained doctors.
D has to train more doctors to develop its infrastructure.

8 Mr. Dubois
A insists that plentiful funds are available for the health service.
B denies that the health service in rural areas is inadequate.
C claims to identify with rural health service problems.
D is initiating policies in the non-metropolitan areas.

Questions on Article C

9 The PM claims
A his country is the most economically stable economy in the region.
B to have overcome the problem of economic instability.
C to have the most developed economy in the region.
D to have developed a successful economy.

10 From his speech we can infer
- *A* agriculture and fisheries are not traditional industries.
- *B* agriculture and fisheries have recovered as a result of their own efforts.
- *C* agriculture and fisheries owe their recovery to government policy.
- *D* most of the government's research funds go into improving traditional industries.

11 He claims that his government have
- *A* increased the standard of living in urban areas.
- *B* increased the standard of living in rural areas.
- *C* built more factories.
- *D* built more houses.

12 According to the PM
- *A* the country areas have been overlooked.
- *B* the country areas are better off than the town areas.
- *C* the entire country is better off.
- *D* the town areas are better off than the country areas.

General questions on all three articles

13 All three articles
- *A* accept the objectives of the RPP.
- *B* admit the limitations of the RPP.
- *C* question the implementation of the RPP.
- *D* defend the implementation of the RPP.

14 In contrast to articles A and C, article B does not mention
- *A* rural living standard.
- *B* the state of the fishing industry.
- *C* health standards.
- *D* employment prospects.

15 The opposition is probably
- *A* urban based.
- *B* rural based.
- *C* regionally based.
- *D* nationally based.

16 In contrast to the writers of articles A and B, the writer of article C is
- *A* pointing out the difficulties faced by the government.
- *B* defending the government's record.
- *C* praising the government's achievements.
- *D* denying the need for a separate RPP policy.

Answers

Section 1

1 *C*
2 *D*
3 *C*
4 *A*
5 *C*
6 *D*
7 *C*
8 *C*
9 *B*
10 *D*
11 *D*

Section 2

1 *B*
2 *D*
3 *A*
4 *A*
5 *C*
6 *D*
7 *B*
8 *A*
9 *C*
10 *D*

Section 3

1 *D*
2 *D*
3 *D*
4 *C*
5 *D*
6 *A*
7 *B*
8 *C*
9 *D*
10 *C*
11 *B*
12 *C*
13 *A*
14 *B*
15 *B*
16 *B*

UNIT 2 · *Arresting stuff*

INTRODUCTION

Violence and crime are features of every society. However, these problems are seen and dealt with in different ways the world over.

The causes and effects of crime are subjects of interest to most, particularly in the light of the rising crime rate in many countries.

This Unit examines various aspects of the topic and makes students aware that a subject can be viewed in very different ways by different groups of people.

OBJECTIVES OF THIS UNIT

Here we are mainly concerned with three things:

1 Teaching students to collect, analyse and present information in an objective and concise manner.

2 Teaching students to understand the organisation of ideas, in particular the relationship of cause and effect, to follow an argument.

3 Teaching students to analyse and respond to an argument in a reasoned way.

SECTION 1 – *SUMMARY*

In this section the general concept of law and order is established. Students are asked to consider how attitudes to the law vary and what the causes and effects of crime are in different countries.

Here students will:

- learn to draft a questionnaire, paying attention to such factors as the purpose of the questionnaire, the size of the sample group, the kind of questions asked, how the answers are noted.
- learn to collect the results of a questionnaire.
- learn to present the results of a questionnaire in tabular or diagrammatic form.

Teaching tips

Page 20

A Question in Students' Book:

– Why do you think laws vary from one society to another?

Students are likely to include the following amongst their answers:

customs of the country
traditions

the country's heritage
prevalent problems of any given society

– What do you think has caused the man in the picture to behave and dress in this way?

No correct answer. Possible answers
– to shock
– to identify with the team he supports
– to be different

– Do you think he represents a threat to order?
No correct answer.

– Explain why behaviour of this kind would or would not be acceptable in your society.
No correct answer.

– Try to list some actions which are legal in the society you are living in but are against the law in other parts of the world.

Students may be encouraged here to list the opposite situation as well, *i.e.* what is illegal in their country and legal elsewhere.

Page 20

B1 The introductory paragraph provides another opportunity to test the students' understanding of the use of figurative language in context. Ask them to read the paragraph and decide on the meaning of the expression 'to turn a blind eye' (= to choose to ignore).

Suggested answers:

a Britain is primarily a Christian country and Sunday, therefore is regarded as 'the day of rest'.

b Watching Sunday sport is not seen as a serious offence.

c There is no correct answer. Some students may argue that committing minor offences will escalate into more serious criminal activities but some students will take the view that people who bend minor laws are unlikely ever to become serious criminals.

Page 21

B2 Questionnaires are a good way of gaining information about people's opinions and form a useful context for practising:

– oral skills
– formulation of questions
– interpretation of data

Before beginning this task it may be useful to revise with the students the present perfect tense, adverbs of frequency such as *always*, *often*, *sometimes*, *occasionally* and *never*.

B3 It is probably not necessary to be too strict about how the students present their data. It is more important to encourage them to develop their own ideas through trial and error and discussion of the effectiveness of their method.

Page 21

B4 To avoid the simple listing of seriousness of offences by, for example, calling out numbers, students should be encouraged to justify the order they suggest. Again, there are no correct answers to the questions, but students with differing opinions should be encouraged to justify their position rather than merely stating it.

Page 22

C1
a Type (*ii*) because it is more 'open'.
b Type (*i*) because it would be presented from a tabular question sheet.
c Type (*i*) because it is a 'closed question' and requires only a tick.
d Type (*i*) because there are only three possible responses.
e Type (*ii*) because it is 'open'.

Page 22

C3 Answers to questions:

I have spilled hot coffee on your arm. It burns you because *it is hot.*
A man steals two TV sets from a warehouse one night. What was his motive? *He intended to sell them.*

The students should draw up a table to be completed like this example:

Car theft			**Shop-lifting**		
Cause	**1**	'Joy-riding'	Cause	**1**	Poverty
	2	Financial gain		**2**	Kleptomania*
	3	Envy		**3**	Financial gain

* psychological affliction where the sufferer steals and hoards things

Note: Students should be concerned with people's motives in committing crimes and should not look for reasons for the incidence of the crimes such as 'unlocked car', 'inadequate store security' and so on.

Page 23

Example for bar graph: the students may decide to take only the first cause to make their graph. In this case the graph would look like this:

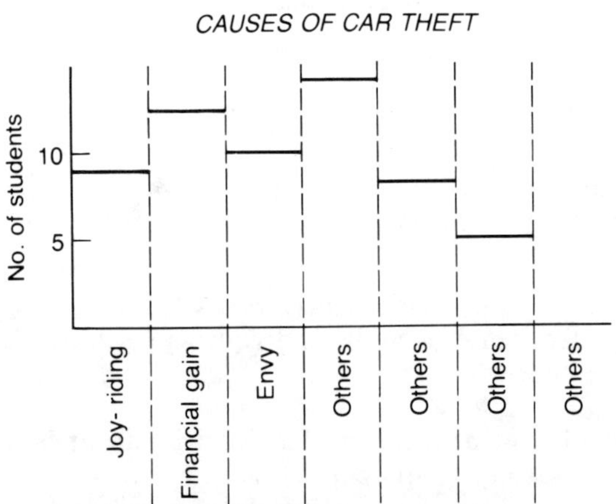

Alternatively, the students may decide to record the causes showing the order of importance. In this case the bar graph might look like this:

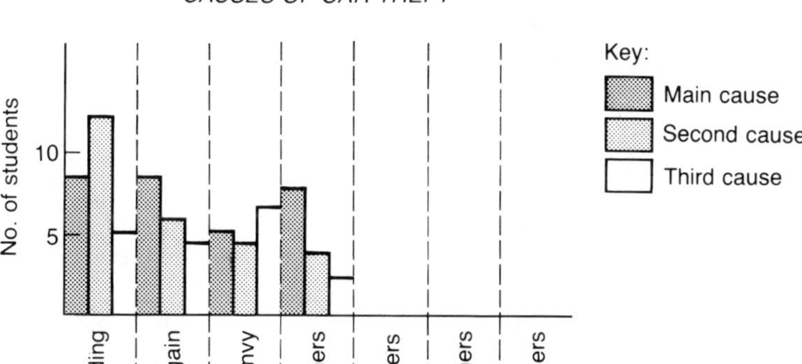

Note: Classification of causes: It is important to ensure that the ways in which different students describe a cause does not result in confusion. For example, 'Financial gain' and 'To sell it' have the same meaning. 'Not enough money' and 'Poverty' must also be classified together.

Answer to question:
– Do you think your results give a reliable indication of wider public opinion? It is likely that the class consists of a group of people of similar age and background and the results therefore may not reflect a wide range of opinion.

Page 23

C4 Students should bear in mind the advantages and disadvantages of the two styles of questionning discussed on the previous page.

Students should try to interview as wide a range of people as possible – members of other classes, teaching staff, family and relations and so on.

For the presentation of the findings, one member of each group should explain who the questionnaire was administered to and how the findings were compiled. Another should report on the actual findings themselves. After all the presentations have been delivered, the class should discuss which technique of *a* compilation and *b* presentation was the most effective and which group delivered their questionnaire to the most representative range of people.

SECTION 2 – *SUMMARY*

In this section students will:

- learn to identify direct cause and effect relationships.
- practise scanning texts for particular information.
- learn to distinguish between objective facts and subjective opinions by:
  a identifying misuse of statistical information.
  b identifying illogicalities in a writer's argument.
- practise presenting a counter-argument in written form.
- practise presenting a paper to a seminar group.

Page 24

A2 It should be pointed out to students that the extract contains views which are offensive to various sectors of society. The authors of this book do not endorse these views. This material is being used to teach the students to recognise bias in writing which claims to be factual.

a This text provides a good opportunity for the students to practise the scanning technique introduced in the previous Unit.
Groups *(iii)*, *(vi)* and *(ix)* are *not* discussed by the author.

b They can then go on to do the note-making task. They might include in their notes:

(i) Crime against people higher than crime against property, especially in summer.

(ii) – In 1924, 31% prisoners sentenced were unemployed.
– Wickersham Commission showed close connection between unemployment and crime.
– 40–50% men admitted to Sing Sing Prison, Feb '29 to Feb '30, unemployed.
– Unemployment leads to crime against property.
– 40% misdemeanor arrests in Cincinatti c. 1929/30 were of unemployed; only 8% of total city population was unemployed.

(iv) – Illiterates much more likely to commit crime than educated people.
– 1923 10.7% prison population illiterate but only 7.1% of general population illiterate.
– Major offenders = higher percentage illiterate.

(v) – 'Strikes productive of crime'.

(vii) – 'Illegitimate children notoriously drift into criminal classes'.

(viii) – More crime, proportionately, in cities than country districts.
– Twice as great a percentage of crime in cities as rural districts.

(x) – U.S. prison census 1939. 51.9% of all prisoners were single; statistics from other countries practically the same.

Page 26

Some students may not immediately be able to identify easily the writer's misuse of statistics and the faulty reasoning he employs. The supplementary exercise should help them to focus on particular points of detail and identify ambiguities.

A3 *b* *(i)* Suggested answer: Because he has strongly held personal opinions.
(v) and *(vi)* If students are unfamiliar with these terms you might use the following exercise.

Ask the students to consult a dictionary to find the meaning of these terms. Then ask them to write contrastive definitions of the two pairs of terms. (This is a good opportunity to practise contrast markers such as *but*, *whereas*, *on the other hand*.)

Here are two examples of the kind of definition students might write:

1 'Subjective' refers to an opinion or personal assessment (possibly based on objective observation) whereas 'objective' refers to something which is verifiable by scientific observation and is not coloured by opinions or emotions.

2 A statistic is a piece of factual information involving mathematical figures, such as ratios, numbers or percentages. A fact is a truth, a real state of things, as opposed to a belief.

Note that the point of **A3** is to focus students' attention on the misuse of statistics by Ellwood. To make sure that they can not only provide good definitions of *subjective*, *objective*, *statistic* and *fact*, you might try to elicit from students the following points in discussion of Ellwood's techniques.

Statistics are commonly regarded as objective facts, but they may be selective in the information they provide or open to misinterpretation leading to false conclusions. Statistics may not give a complete picture and thus their 'objectivity' is reduced.

In the Ellwood article, the author uses statistics to reinforce subjective opinions. The conclusions he draws are not valid from the statistical information he uses. An analysis of the prison population gives information about the criminals who are caught, not the extent or causes of crime.

Supplementary exercises

1 On page 25 the writer says that in 1939 51.9% of all prisoners were single. This seems quite a high figure and appears to support his view that single people are more likely to commit crimes than married people. However, if we turn the figures round we see that 48.1% of prisoners in 1939 were either married or divorced. This provides a very different picture.

Read through the text and see if you can identify any other examples where you can turn the statistics the other way round.

2 Statistics are not the only way that the writer is able to give a false impression to the reader. For instance, when reading the text we can find many examples where he seems to be suggesting something he is unable to provide any proof for.

Read the relevant parts of the text to explain why he is unable to justify the following statements.

a People living in warm climates commit more crimes against the person than people living in cold climates.

b 85–90% of children from demoralised or disrupted homes go to reform schools for delinquent children. Around 50% of criminals come from the unemployed class.

Suggested answers:

1 Students may suggest some of the following:
- 50–60% of all men admitted to Sing-Sing Prison in the year ending Feb 28, 1930 were employed.
- The 1923 prison census showed that 69% of prisoners committed in that year were employed.
- The 1923 prison census showed that 90.3% of prisoners were literate.

2 *a* Although he suggests that crimes against the person in warm climates are common he never at any time compares their incidence to the number of crimes actually occurring against the person in cold climates.

b 85– 90% of the children in delinquent schools are from broken homes but they may be a very small percentage of the total number of children from disrupted homes who live perfectly ordinary lives.

Although the writer says that 50% of all convicted criminals are unemployed this does not mean that 50% of all crimes are committed by employed people. It may mean that the unemployed do not have the same resources to escape detection which a wealthier person may have.

Page 26

A4 From the above investigation of Ellwood's techniques, the students should now be in a position to assemble strong and coherent arguments against Ellwood. In doing this it is obviously of basic importance that they do not employ any of the questionable tactics he adopted.

The students' arguments:

– should contain no contradictions or illogicalities.
– should use statistics accurately and appropriately.
– may contain subjective views but these should not be presented as objective statements.

A5 In preparing the paper, it is essential that the students accurately set out Ellwood's views before going on to criticise them. This is to avoid the danger of falsely attributing ideas to other people.

Page 26

B1 In further education, the students will almost certainly have the opportunity to take part in seminars. They will definitely be obliged to attend tutorials.

You may find it useful to discuss with your students the difference between the two. (A tutorial involves a smaller number of people; usually one student reads out a paper which he/she has written; the contents of the paper are then discussed by the group. The objective is not necessarily to develop new ideas but is generally to synthesise existing views.)

Difference between seminar/debate: This provides a further opportunity for students to practise writing contrastive definitions. They may write something like the following:

The participants in a seminar seek to work towards general agreement, whereas in a debate one side is seeking to totally refute the arguments of the other.

Page 27

B2 Before the seminar begins, point out to the students that they are to take accurate notes which they must use in the subsequent discussion. The objective is that they use them to distinguish clearly between (*i*) Ellwood's views and (*ii*) the respective view of each speaker during the presentations and (*iii*) their own views.

SECTION 3 – *SUMMARY*

In this section students will:

– practise guessing the meaning of words from context.
– practise identifying causes and effects in reading and listening.
– practise organising notes.
– practise using notes to write a short essay.
– practise analysing an argument.
– learn to infer the opinion of a writer.
– practise writing a short essay describing causes and effects of a problem.

Teaching tips

Page 27

A1 If you think students will have difficulty with this task, show them how it is sometimes possible to work out the meaning of unknown words by using clues in the text. For example, let us look at the word *layman* in the introduction to this exercise. The context is the explanation of crime; experts are seen sometimes to have difficulty in finding an explanation. The word *alike* shows us that both expert and layman have difficulty. We can see that experts and laymen are different groups of people. Thus a layman is someone who is not an expert. Suggest that the students apply these steps to establishing the meaning of the expressions 'mummy's boy' and 'ran amok'.

Supplementary exercise

The article 'Mummy's boy who ran amok' can provide valuable practice in identifying and recording new vocabulary.

Ask students to read through the article and identify all the words and phrases the writer uses to:

- describe Michael Ryan's interests.
- describe Michael Ryan's relationships.
- describe Michael Ryan's personality.

Then note down all the words and phrases with a column for each heading.

Students should include all or most of the following vocabulary:

Interests	**Relationships**	**Personality**
– kept a formidable armoury of guns – tended them the way most people tend plants – best clothes, fastest cars, latest records – owned an antique gun shop – new car he would appear with each year – clothes and guns – Labrador dog Blackie – with the dog every evening – go for a drive in the evening – teenage boys would kick a football on the common with Ryan	– only child – father died two years ago – idolised by mother – close relationship with dog – 'only one I saw him with was his mum.' – played football with teenage boys	– shy 27-year-old – polite – mummy's boy – solitariness – 'you never saw him with friends.' – 'totally unremarkable.' – 'used to shout at kids if they went up his driveway.'

– member of a shooting club

The dividing line between relationships and personality is very slight and you should not be too worried if students have mixed entries for these categories.

When students have completed the table ask them to write a short description of Michael Ryan, taking into account the characteristics mentioned above.

After they have completed this task ask them to compare it with the description they wrote on page 11 of Unit 1.

- What are the objectives of the writer in each case?
- What examples can you find of negative and positive use of language?

Students should be aware that in the first passage they are describing somebody that they probably respect and admire whereas in the second, somebody is being described in a critical and unflattering manner.

Page 28

A2 Suggested answers:

- single person (although living in familiar environment)
- unemployed (although not poor)
- 'socially abnormal' (did not mix, few friends, always alone)
- 'influence of . . . the motion picture' (Rambo – a violent film character who solves problems with a gun)

Page 28

A3 You might point out to the students that as experts are unable to provide a solution, any idea the class may have can only be speculative. However, they may mention some of the following:

- only child.
- 'spoilt' by mother.
- 'never grew up'.
- unemployed.
- age difference
  - (i) between parents
  - (ii) between father and son
- not the western norm.
- lived in fantasy world.
- obsession with guns.

Note: Of course not all single, mother-dominated, unemployed men who are interested in guns turn into violent killers.

A4 It is important that students can distinguish between what the government does in the aftermath of this particular tragedy and what it can do to prevent similar incidents occurring in the future. Obviously, only certain things are within the government's control. For instance, they cannot force people to get married or make people have friends.

There is no single correct answer here. Any factors mentioned which the government can influence are acceptable. Two possibilities are tighter control of gun laws and stricter surveillance of gun club membership.

Page 28

B2 Although the government did not consider stricter surveillance of gun club membership this is not to say that it was not an intelligent prediction of **A4** above.

Note: If students mention 'talks between BBC and ITV on screen violence', they should be reminded that these organisations are not entirely government controlled.

B3 *a* Possible answers

- over-exciting
- fanatical support
- over-crowding
- use of alcohol
- rivalry between supporters

c Possible answers

- English most violent
- worst (and longest) reputation

B4 The tapescript can be found on page 150 of this book.

a Students' notes should include some of the following:

(*i*) **Cause**	**Effect**
Heysel	Popplewell Committee
violence of matches	membership scheme
membership scheme	ban on 'away' supporters
ban on 'away' supporters	unfair advantage to 'home' team
introduction of computerized membership cards	increase of crowd control
	absence of violence
introduction of membership scheme	fewer police required
	reduced size of crowd
(*ii*) **Problem**	**Solution**
football violence	100% membership scheme ban on away supporters computerized membership card withdrawal of membership card for bad behaviour
townspeople disturbed by visiting supporters	visiting supporters banned

If students encounter difficulties identifying Cause/Effect and Problem/Solution relationships, you might stop the tape and demonstrate to them one or two early examples. If a student points out the difficulties of the 'good' supporter not being able to attend games, you should explain that Dr. Foster does not regard this as a problem and hence proposes no solution.

Page 29

B4*b* In topics (*i*) and (*ii*) Cause/Effect notes will be relevant. In (*iii*) and (*iv*) Problem/Solution notes should be used.

This exercise which practises transferring information from note-form to full written form, provides an opportunity for the students to assess whether their notes are comprehensive and tidy enough to be used even by other people. It is also a context for the students to get more practice in using the language of cause and effect (verbs or markers) in addition to language associated with problems and solution (mainly verbs – such as: *propose/implement/solve/deal with/rectify/overcome*).

Example (Cause/Effect):
'As a result of Luton Town's ban on away fans the problem of violence at matches has been removed resulting in a reduction in the number of police required. It has also, however, reduced attendances at home matches.'

Example (Problems/Solution):
'The 100% membership scheme has dealt with the problem of football violence by banning 'away' fans and withdrawing the membership of badly behaved 'home' supporters.'

Page 30

D The students' attention is drawn to the importance of being able to detect hidden meaning as it is critical that they develop the skill of identifying a writer's opinion or viewpoint in order to assess the conclusions he may arrive at. Students should appreciate that it is not only when confronted by an author whose opinions they disagree with that this skill is important. Even when the writer's and reader's opinions agree, the subject material may be presented in a way that assumes a degree of subject knowledge beyond the reader's. In this case the reader has to be able to infer to acquire the 'missing' information.

D1 *a and b* Here the students are guided through the basic steps involved in making an inference.

Page 31

D2 In texts 1 to 4 students should look at the questions first and answer them as they read the relevant sections of each.

(General comment on the texts: this method of answering questions is intended to get the students used to looking for clues to unstated opinion as they read. By text 5 it is hoped they will be able to make the main inferences without this assistance.)

Page 33

D3 Each group should work on **one** of the texts 6 to 9.
They should discuss any possible inferences which the text presents.

D3 *b* To monitor their progress, you might move from group to group and ask them to explain and justify the inferences they have made.

Supplementary exercises

Although students have spent a long time examining these texts intensely the following supplementary exercise may be useful. It shows them that the way a reader approaches a text can vary dramatically according to his or her objectives.

For these questions you will need to look through texts 5–8 on pages 33–34 again.

1 Which text makes most reference to statistics?
A Text 5 C Text 7
B Text 6 D Text 8

2 Which text is least subjective?
A Text 5 C Text 7
B Text 6 D Text 8

3 Which text makes most reference to the effects of drinking?
A Text 5 C Text 7
B Text 6 D Text 8

4 Which text proposes a definite solution?
A Text 5 C Text 7
B Text 6 D Text 8

Answers: **1** B **2** B **3** C **4** A

Page 34

D4 When preparing written assignments, students often make the mistake of not letting their reader know that some of their information is 'borrowed' from other sources. Using other sources is, of course, perfectly permissible but the student who does not somehow acknowledge 'borrowing' runs the risk of:

(*i*) being accused of plagiarism (stealing other people's ideas).
Plagiarism involves making major unattributed use of someone else's ideas and as such is looked down on in academic circles. It is usually avoided by naming the source, either in the text or by reference to a bibliography.

(*ii*) implying that he accepts views with which he does not in fact wish to be associated.
Associating oneself with these views is not an offence but it is obviously not in the writer's interests to allow this to happen as it could cause serious illogicalities in his argument.

You might discuss the above points with your class before you begin this exercise. This is an important area, especially for students already involved in, or soon to be involved in, further education.

a Ask the students whether they think the writer is making major use of someone else's ideas or wishing to dissociate himself from someone else's views.
- The writer uses the inverted commas to show that these are someone else's words.
- From what we see in the rest of the text we can safely assume the writer does not agree with the view they express.

  Other ways of indicating the use of outside sources might include: using expressions like

  - as X says, . . .
  - according to X, . . .
  - in the words of X, . . .
  - to quote X, . . .
  - X states that . . .
  - X claims that . . .

b In their articles students should be encouraged to show where they have used other people's words or views.

c When the students have reviewed each other's work, you might elicit from the class all the ways they used to indicate their use of other people's opinions and write these on the blackboard.

SECTION 4 – *SUMMARY*

In this section students will be engaged in:

- conducting a formal meeting, including:
  the preparation of an agenda
  the briefing of the chairperson and secretary
  notes on conduct
- examining a selection of texts for information relevant to a particular topic.

Teaching tips

It should be stressed to students that this activity differs from similar sections in later Units. They have to play the role of another person and put forward opinions which are not their own. Students may resist this approach seeing it as make believe.

It may help to improve their motivation if you point out that the skill of being able to stick to a brief is a very useful one. The application for law students of course is a direct one but students of any discipline must be able to articulate the views of leading authorities in their field.

Procedure for this activity This is the crucial part of the whole role-play. When students have decided upon their own role they **must** meet with the members of other groups who have chosen the same role as themselves. In this discussion they should reach agreement on a standard course of action to follow in their 'meetings' with the rest of their groups.

Point out to the students that the viewpoints held by the various members of the company are not totally distinct and it may be necessary to form alliances with other members of the company. This will be particularly important if the chairperson decides to take a vote on the matter.

Follow-up discussion Before the follow-up discussions, point out to the students that there is no obvious and commonly accepted solution. What they must consider is why several groups of people began from a similar starting point and arrived at a varied set of solutions. Their attention should be drawn to considering what enables some people to persuade others of the correctness of their own point of view and where others might improve in this direction.

SECTION 5

There is a great danger that students may neglect this section. Consequently, it is a good idea if they carry out the first attempt of these presentations within the lesson under your supervision. Thereafter they should be able to continue to practise the skills unaided.

If students have difficulty in choosing suitable topics you may refer them to their subject teachers. Remember it is not your job to correct the students' opinions on specialist matters. Try to concentrate on the ways they make use of language in order to put forward those views.

TEST PRACTICE

The following questions have been provided on the work in this Unit. Students will need a multiple-choice answer sheet and copies of questions 1–28 which follow. Teachers should read the script beginning on page 161 before giving the test.

Listening This is a test of your ability to understand spoken English.

Section 1

Listen to your teacher and make a suitable choice from the alternatives given.

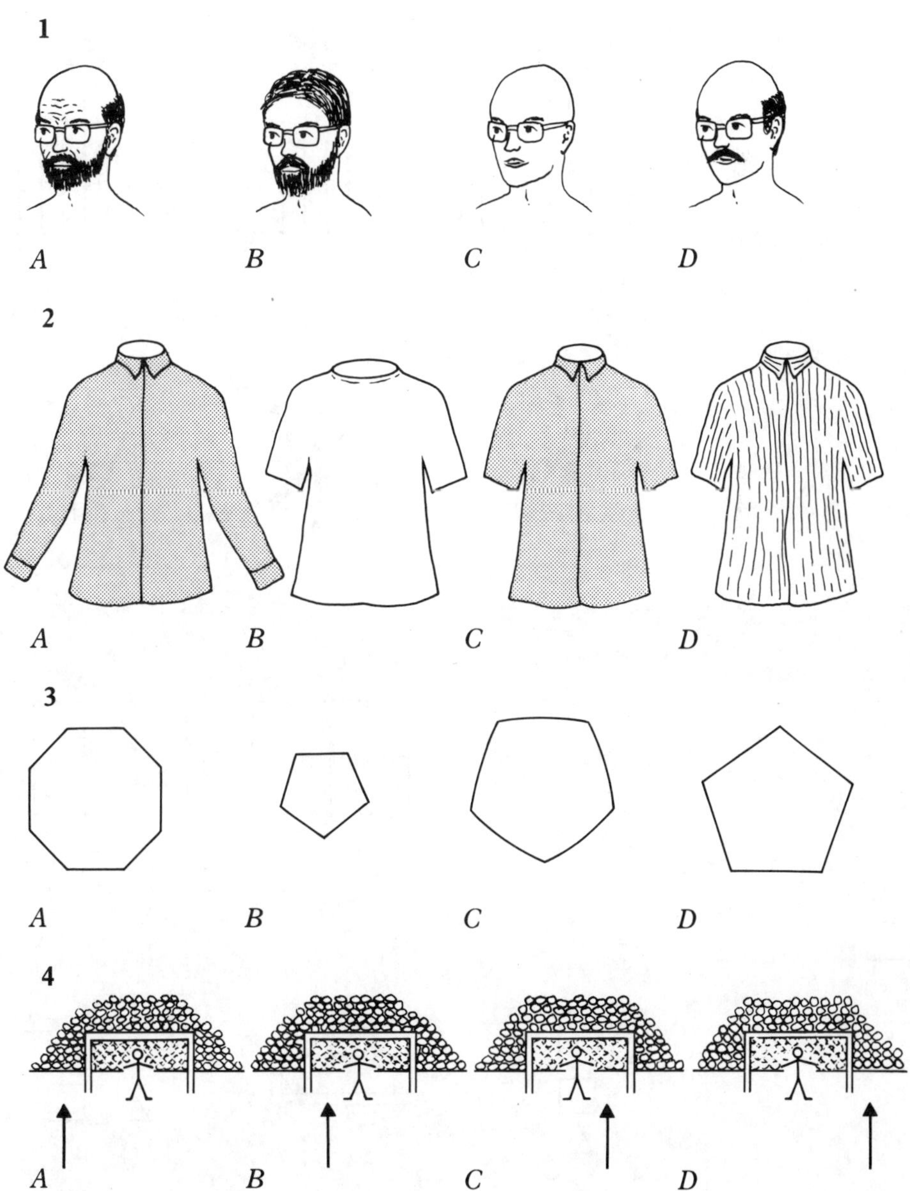

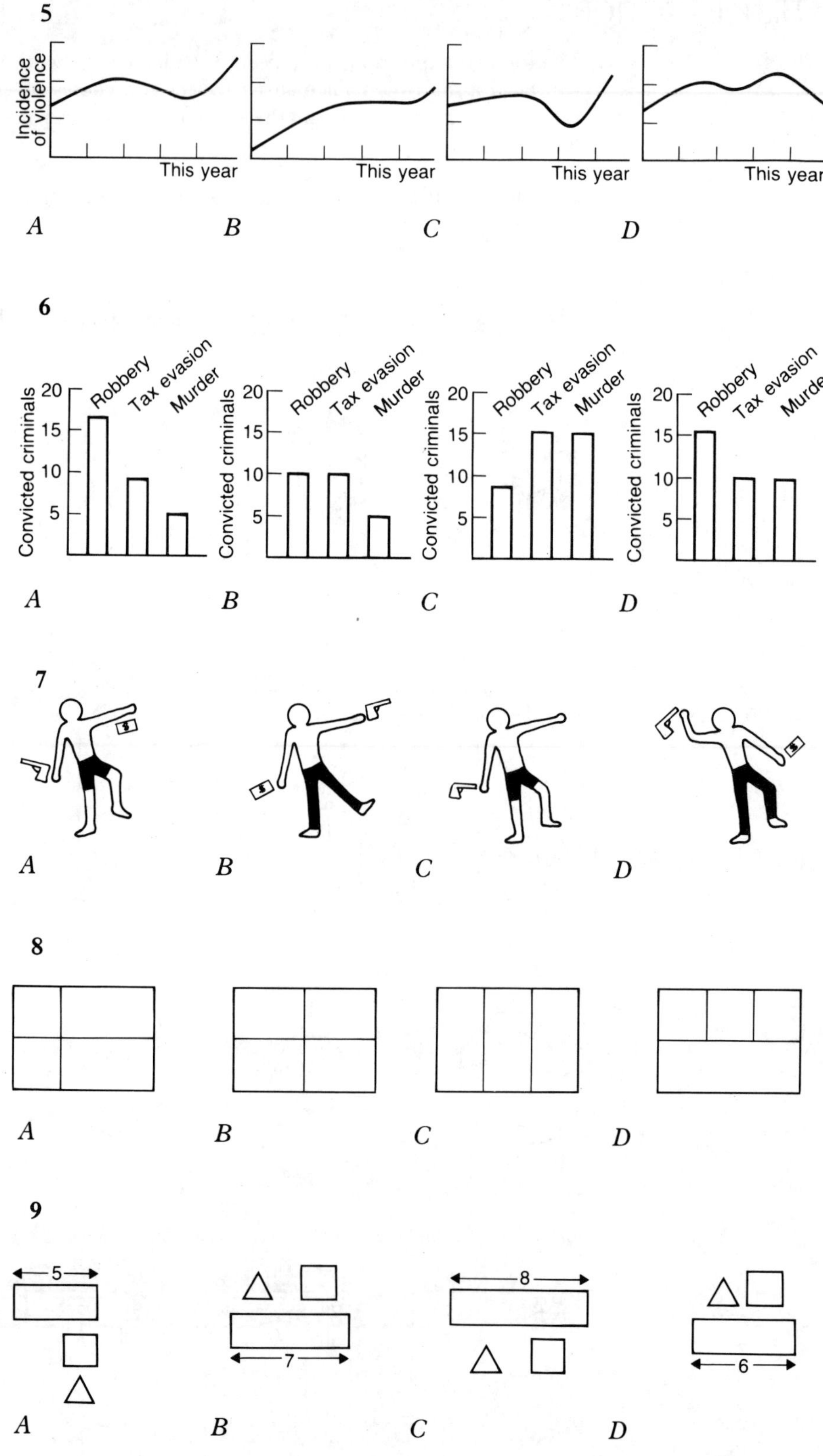
5
Incidence of violence
This year
This year
This year
This year
A
B
C
D
6
Convicted criminals
Robbery
Tax evasion
Murder
20
15
10
5
A
B
C
D
7
A
B
C
D
8
A
B
C
D
9
5
7
8
6
A
B
C
D

10

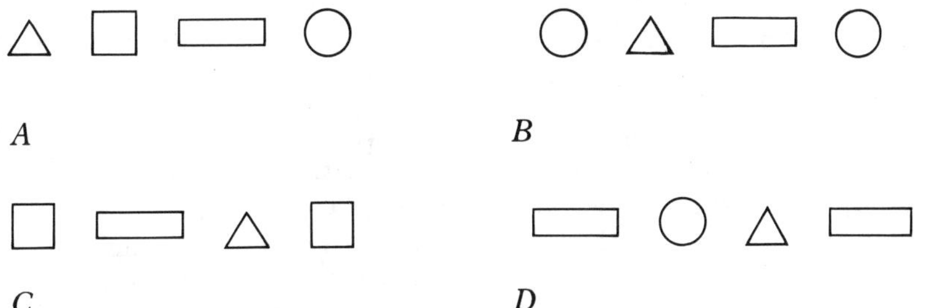

Section 2

Listen again to the Unit 2 interview on the tape. You will hear the interview only once.

Join the club

11 Which of the following statements most accurately describes the government's current position on membership of football clubs?
A They are considering the compulsory introduction of a 100% membership scheme.
B They have decided to introduce a compulsory 100% membership scheme.
C They no longer want to introduce a 100% membership scheme.
D They are no longer going to introduce a 100% membership scheme.

12 Who does Dr. Foster blame for the non-introduction of a compulsory 100% membership scheme?
A The hooligans.
B The Government.
C The Football Authorities
D Luton Town.

13 One of the disadvantages of the 100% membership scheme is
A that membership is only compulsory for 50% of a club's supporters.
B football hooligans can still join.
C the ban on away fans gives the home team an unfair advantage.
D it doesn't reduce the level of violence at matches.

14 What is a Luton supporter able to do?
A See a match for a pound.
B Buy season tickets in advance.
C Pay for tickets by credit card.
D Use his membership card to pay for tickets.

15 Which type of person does Dr. Foster show the most concern for?
A Non-violent footballers.
B Non-football supporters.
C Non-violent football supporters.
D Violent football supporters.

16 Which adjective best represents Dr. Foster's attitude?
A Convinced.
B Pessimistic.
C Unreasonable.
D Resigned.

17 Dr. Foster agrees that
A fewer supporters are going to watch matches.
B the membership scheme is intimidating to the man in the street.
C the membership scheme is not working.
D it's more difficult for genuine supporters to watch the game.

18 Dr. Foster believes
A 50% membership schemes are more successful.
B membership schemes are unsuccessful.
C 100% membership schemes are more successful.
D football is a majority sport.

Section 3 – Appropriate responses

Your teacher will read aloud comments from Denis Fairchild's colleagues discussing the circumstances behind his arrest. As you listen, choose the response you think is most appropriate.

19 *A* This time last year.
B Two million dollars.
C Before the holidays.
D Since he started here.

20 *A* Oh yes, at least three thousand dollars.
B He won't offer to resign.
C If they think he is innocent.
D It depends on the evidence.

21 *A* About seven days.
B Everyone in the department.
C I'm not sure.
D More than I can stand.

22 *A* In used notes.
B By car.
C Badly.
D She's a widow, you know.

23 *A* Yes, he did.
B He didn't need the money.
C I don't know.
D He programmed the computer to issue cheques to fictitious companies.

24 *A* A clerk noticed a cheque for a large amount.
B Only by accident.
C A few months ago.
D The police arrested him for embezzlement.

25 *A* The judge is sympathetic.
B He was charged with embezzlement.
C About two years.
D He won't get away with it.

26 *A* He came from quite a rich family.
B He got on well with his colleagues.
C Yes, he never used to do much work.
D Not particularly, but he had a BMW and a Porsche.

27 *A* More than $200,000.
B He's probably spent it by now.
C They'll never get it back.
D His wife's got a new fur coat.

28 *A* Computer fraud is difficult to detect.
B He'd been doing it for years.
C He got caught in the end.
D He didn't get away with it.

UNIT 3 · *A question of power*

INTRODUCTION

Most people are familiar with the more conventional sources of energy which we rely on. Depleting oil supplies and the ill effects of coal burning are popular subjects of discussion. But how many people know about drawing heat from the earth's core, using mirrors to boil tanks of water or harnessing the tides to drive turbines?

And what exactly do people know about nuclear power, other than that it is efficient but risky?

This unit offers a deeper look at issues which are highly topical now and promise to be of even greater importance in the future. It also attempts to sharpen readers' critical faculties when they are confronted with texts on these issues.

OBJECTIVES OF THIS UNIT

Here we are mainly concerned with:

1 Teaching students to select and note relevant points from reading and listening for re-use.
2 Teaching students to arrive at solutions through reasoned comparison and contrast of the facts and details.
Throughout the Unit a number of other study and exam skills are taught and practised. These are listed below, section by section.

SECTION 1 – *SUMMARY*

In this section students will have the opportunity to take a broad look at current issues concerning the question of energy.
Students will:

- practise listening to a realistic talk for particular information.
- learn to identify the main areas of a talk and formulate headings for notes.
- learn to use suitable note-taking techniques for listening such as *a* outlining and *b* key words.

Teaching tips

Page 45
As a warm-up activity, you could ask the students:

– What energy sources do these headlines refer to?

More information about many of these sources is contained in the unit. At this stage there is no need to correct or add to students' ideas. This is only a device to get them thinking about sources in preparation for **A**. So keep it short.

Headlines	**Explanation**
Oil price ups and downs	refers to variations in the cost of oil.
Power from hot rocks	refers to geothermal energy, which involves extracting heat from the earth.
Finding alternatives	could refer to alternatives to conventional energy sources. Commonly discussed alternatives are solar, wind and tidal power.
Radioactive food turns up in Malaysia Chernobyl: countdown to catastrophe	Both refer to the accident that occurred at a nuclear power plant in the USSR in 1986. The cloud of radio-active dust contaminated a lot of food.
Solar villages planned for Ladakh	refers to plans to provide energy to villages in the north of India using the sun as the energy source.
Power from the farmers	refers to the possibility of using crops for energy, for example by burning crop waste or by making alcohol from it, as is done with sugarcane in Brazil.
Acid Rain	refers to the results of pollutants in the air being carried by clouds and eventually released as rain with a high acidic content. This rain damages forests, fisheries and buildings. Coal fired power stations have been blamed for this problem.

Page 45

A1–5 You might have students deal with these discussion questions in small groups.

Insist that all students note down the ideas the group comes up with. This is important for the first listening task in **B**. Have each group report back to the class briefly, using their notes.

Page 46

B1 involves using the notes from **A** as a checklist for what the speaker says.

Before playing the tape make sure students are clear about what they are going to do, and how they are going to mark their notes. *e.g.* tick, underline, asterisk, etc.

Play tape once.

You could ask students for a quick, round the class feedback on points they have marked. This will help weaker students who might have missed a few points, to keep up with the rest.

Page 46

B2 In the previous exercise, students were only asked to match words or ideas that they heard with their own list. In **B2**, they are performing a more difficult task in that they have to understand the context of the listening, then compare this with the situation in their own country.

To ensure that students can do this, it will be necessary to check that they have understood what the speaker has said about the world situation. If teachers feel that the understanding is shaky, try the following exercise.

Supplementary exercise

Write the following series of sentences on the blackboard.
Tell students to look at them and decide if they are true or false.
Play the tape and ask students to check their answers.

1 The world is definitely facing an energy crisis, according to the speaker.
(False – The world may be facing difficulties, but not necessarily a crisis.)

2 The speaker says that the world depends mainly on five energy sources.
(True – They are oil, coal, gas, hydro-electric power and nuclear power.)

3 The speaker claims that the advantages of nuclear power far outweigh its disadvantages.
False – The speaker is concerned about the disadvantages *e.g.* safety.)

4 The speaker maintains that there is nothing to be gained from nuclear power.
(False – The speaker lists the advantages of nuclear power *e.g.* the small amount of fuel needed, cheap running costs, fuel easily transported, little pollution, high efficiency in electricity production)

5 The speaker does not believe that the oil industry is on the decline.
True – She feels that there are still large reserves of oil, as well as coal and gas (fossil fuels).

6 The speaker is not very optimistic about the future of alternative energy sources.
True – She feels that cost, public opinion, geographical factors may cause problems.

7 Possible alternative energy sources for the future are solar, OTEC, tidal, hydro-electric, geothermal, gas.
False – Hydro-electric power and gas are considered to be conventional sources in that they are already used to produce large amounts of electricity.

This exercise provides an opportunity to check students' understanding of vocabulary associated with energy *e.g.* fossil fuels, conventional/alternative sources, etc.

Page 46

B3 If you feel that students will find this exercise difficult, try stopping the tape at the asterisks in the tapescript and ask students to suggest headings.
You may elicit similar ideas to this:

***1** Energy problems?
***2** Most common world sources
***3** Problems of nuclear power
***4** Advantages of nuclear power
***5** The future of conventional sources
***6** Alternative sources

Page 47

C3 This additional checklist might help students when comparing notes.

> **Checklist for notes**
> **1** Do your notes make use of main headings?
> **2** Is it easy to distinguish small details from the main headings?
> **3** Are the notes pleasant to look at?
> **4** Would you be able to understand them in a month from now?

Stress that the most important thing is that students are able to understand their own notes. But they must also feel that they will be useful in the future. Scribbled and untidy notes should be discouraged, as no-one will want to read them again.

SECTION 2 – *SUMMARY*

In this section we take a closer look at renewable sources of energy, most of which are alternative sources, and we learn a little more about the way they work, their advantages and their disadvantages.

Students will:

- learn to pick out similarities and differences between two systems.
- learn to summarise similarities and differences in note form on a grid.
- practise formulating headings for notes.
- practise scanning long texts for specific information.
- practise asking for specific information.
- learn the language necessary to compare and contrast.
- learn to write summaries working from notes in grid form.

Page 48

A1 If students do not seem to be clear as to what renewable energy sources are, try the following exercise.

Supplementary exercise

Put the lists of words below on the blackboard. Ask students to decide what the differences are between the two groups of words.

Write the heading 'Renewable Sources' over the left-hand group and ask students for a heading for the right-hand group.

Point out that 'Conventional Sources' is not acceptable as hydro-electric power is in the other group.

Point out that 'Alternative Sources' is not acceptable, since some of these are conventional.

Elicit the heading 'Non-Renewable Sources'.

1 What are the major differences between these two groups of words?

tidal	oil
geothermal	coal
hydro-electric	gas
solar	peat
O.T.E.C.	nuclear
wind	

2 Find a heading for each group.

Page 48

B1 Students will probably have little difficulty in listing the details of similarity and difference between the two sources (*e.g.* renewable, widely used, undeveloped, near water, lakes/estuaries, expensive, cheap power, etc.)

However, now they are required to classify these details under headings.

e.g.	**Detail**	**Heading**
	expensive/cheap	costs – capital – generating
	rivers/estuaries	location

Use these examples if students are having difficulty in understanding what is required.

Page 49

B4 Students may be tempted to write full sentences. Discourage them from doing this.

C4 This activity is an important one. It encourages students to share information, rather than to rely solely on the original source.

Encourage students to ask appropriate questions, and if necessary to follow up questions to get all the information they require.

Supplementary exercise

If you feel that your students need practice in this type of question-making, try the following exercise.

Stage 1 – Straightforward questions

Tell students to look at the grid on page 49. Ask them what questions they would ask to find out that information.

Probably students will come up with questions like these.

1 What is the importance of H.E.P. on a world scale?
2 What is a suitable location?
3 Where is it currently exploited?
4 What is the capital outlay for an H.E.P. plant?
5 What are the generating costs?
6 What is the life expectancy of an H.E.P. plant?
7 What are the advantages of H.E.P.?
8 What are the disadvantages of H.E.P.?

Stage 2 – varied question forms

Such question forms are perfectly acceptable. However, you may want your students to be able to vary the way they ask questions to avoid monotony.

Ask the students for other ways of seeking the same information. For example, you might expect:

1 How important is H.E.P. on a world scale?
or Compared with other energy sources, how important is this one?
2 What kind of places do you find H.E.P. stations in?
or What would be a suitable place to build an H.E.P. plant?
3 Do you find H.E.P. plants in many countries?
or In what countries can H.E.P. stations be found?

4 How much investment is necessary to build H.E.P. stations?
or Do you have any figures for capital outlay for H.E.P. plants?
5 Can these plants produce power cheaply?
or How do generating costs in this type of plant compare with those of other sources?
6 How long is it estimated that this type of plant will last?
or What kind of lifespan has this plant type got?
7/8 Does this energy source have any advantages/disadvantages as regards safety/pollution/the environment?
or What are transmission costs like?

Stage 3 – polite questions

If students are able to vary their questions, but fail to use polite, tentative forms, encourage them to consider ways of doing this.

Ask students to examine the question forms of Stage 1 and/or 2 and to suggest phrases that could be added to make them more polite.

Possible suggestions are:

a Can/Could you tell me ..?
b Do you happen to know ..?
c Have you any idea ..?
d Do you know anything about ..?

Point out to students how these additions can change the form of a question.
e.g. What are the generating costs? – Could you tell me what the generating costs are?
Additions *b* and *c* have the same effect.

What is the capital outlay? – Do you know anything about capital outlay?

'About' is followed by a noun phrase.

Pages 50–54
The texts on these pages contain technical, semi-technical and general vocabulary which some students may find difficult. It is important to note that students do not need to understand all this vocabulary in order to complete **C** on page 49. However, the teacher may want to exploit these texts further and from them teach some useful general vocabulary.

Supplementary exercise

Put the headings and the focus words from the table below on the blackboard.

Focus words	Possible associated words	Associated words in texts	Meaning or synonym
exploit (ed) (able)	workers mine energy	energy	use

Focus words	Possible associated words	Associated words in texts	Meaning or synonym
generate/ generation	energy power electricity gap	electricity	produce or make production
turbine	turn dam power generator water	spin generate electricity vapour drives	generator wheel
output	electricity power energy	peak 4 kw power plant	volume of production
transmit	energy power heat	heat	carry
plant	power generating equipment	geothermal large situated area	building
scale	world large small	on a large on a small use	extent of a project size
capital	outlay money	costs investment	fixed or plant costs – opposite to running costs

Ask students to jot down words or phrases they would expect to find associated with these focus words.
Suggestions for the teacher's reference are included here. The students may come up with different answers.

Now ask students to refer to the text they read, either *Solar Energy* or *Geothermal Power*, and locate as many of these focus words as they can.
Tell them to note down associated words they actually find in the text in the third column.

Working from the table, ask students to suggest an explanation or synonym for each focus word and note these in the fourth column. Suggestions are included above.
Encourage students to use a dictionary to check or find answers.

Finally, ask students to examine their texts for other words and

phrases which they feel they need to understand.
Limit the number of words and stress that they must be vital for comprehension of the text.
Ask students to extend their table to include their chosen words.
Then they should complete the table in the same way and compare their results.

The teacher may feel that students need more work on the language of comparison and contrast before they attempt the writing task. If so, try the following exercises.

Supplementary exercise

1 Similarities

A If you consider your grid and the grid in the book you will notice some striking similarities between hydro-electric power and geothermal power.
Indicate on your grid in which areas this is so.
Now consider the following sentence halves and match them.

1 Both hydro-electric power and geothermal power
2 Like hydro-electric power, geothermal power
3 Electricity generating costs
4 As regards large scale production
5 H.E.P. and geothermal power are similar
6 Neither hydro-electric power

U in that they could be exploited on a world-wide basis
V nor geothermal power is expensive in terms of running costs, by comparison with the more conventional sources.
W also requires large amounts of capital outlay.
X geothermal power is just as suitable for this as H.E.P.
Y can be classed as renewable energies.
Z are low in both cases.

(Answers: **1 Y 2 W 3 Z 4 X 5 U 6 V**)

B There are also a number of similarities between H.E.P. and tidal power.
Again indicate where this is so on your grid.
Then look at the example below and make sentences in the same way.

Example: Use water to produce electricity (Both ... and ...)
Both tidal and H.E.P. schemes use water to produce electricity.

1 Renewable energy source (Both ... and ...)
2 Capital costs (In both cases ...)
3 Running costs (... just as ... as)
4 Risk to life (Neither ... nor ...)
5 Lifespan of the plant (Like)

C Now using information from the grid, write five sentences describing

similarities between any of the energy sources. Your sentences may be true or false.
Read your sentences to your partner and have him/her decide whether they are true or not.

2 Differences

A Having looked at some of the similarities between power sources, let us now consider some of the differences.
Read through the following list of statements and note down whether they are true or false.
If they are false, can you correct them?

1 Geothermal schemes are not nearly as common as H.E.P. schemes at the moment.
2 H.E.P. is considerably more expensive in terms of generating costs than geothermal power.
3 Geothermal plants differ from H.E.P. plants in that they have a much longer life span.
4 The prospects for producing geothermal energy on a small scale are poor, whereas H.E.P. is very suitable for small scale production.
5 Unlike H.E.P. schemes, geothermal plants have the capacity to provide a number of other services apart from electricity supply, such as irrigation, flood control and water supply.
6 H.E.P. is already an important and established source of energy. On the other hand, geothermal energy is still very much at the experimental stage.

(Answers: **1T 2F 3F 4T 5F 6T**)

B Using information from the grid in the students' book and from your own grids, complete the following sentences in any way you wish.

1 Hydro-electric schemes are much more suitable for small scale development than ...
2 H.E.P. plants already produce vast quantities of power in several countries. On the other hand ...
3 Unlike tidal stations where output varies according to the tide ...
4 Hydro-electric power and tidal power differ in that tidal power relies on the movement of the tides, while H.E.P. ...
5 Environmental problems associated with H.E.P. stations concern flooding of agricultural land and change of climate, while ...
6 Whereas tidal power is limited to a small number of suitable sites, ...

C This exercise makes use of the diagrams below.
Divide the class into two groups, A and B. Students in group A should be given the upper pair of diagrams, while group B should receive the lower pair.

Each group should write a series of sentences describing the similarities and differences between the two dams they have diagrams of, using the phrases they have been practising. This could be done as individual work, but might be more fun if done as a group activity.

The groups should swap their sentences, but not their diagrams, and using this information, try to draw a sketch of the third dam.

Allow the groups to see each others' results and ask them to decide what has caused any inaccuracies.

Were the describing sentences not exact enough, or not complete enough? Or did the sketchers fail to extract enough information from the sentences?

Group A

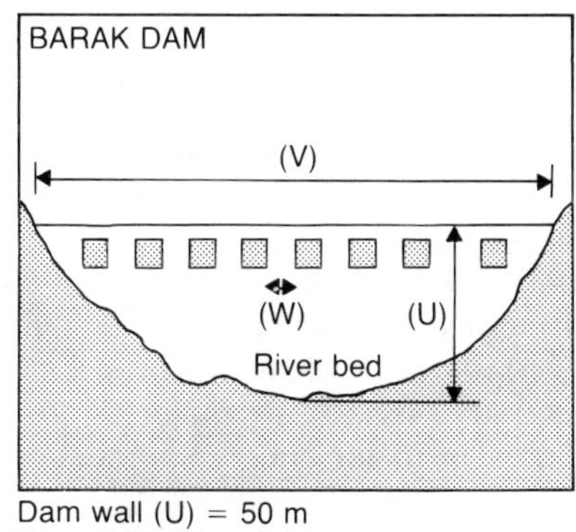

Dam wall (U) = 50 m
Dam width (V) = 1.5 km
Distance between sluices (W) = 150 m

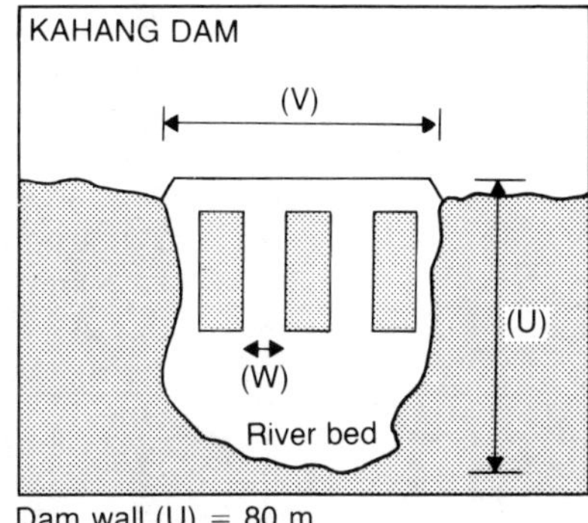

Dam wall (U) = 80 m
Dam width (V) = 400 m
Distance between sluices (W) = 60 m

Group B

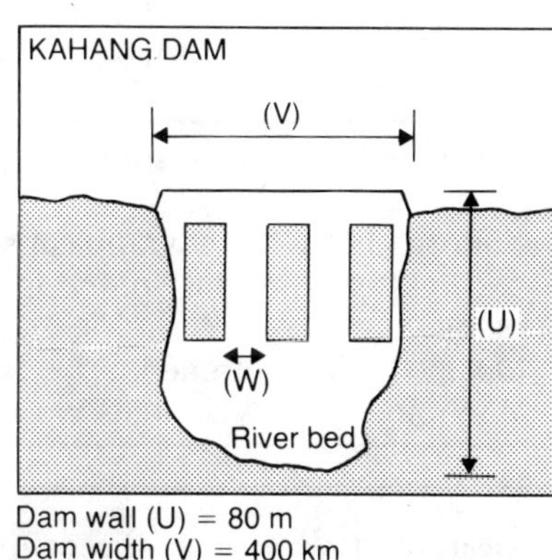

Dam wall (U) = 80 m
Dam width (V) = 400 km
Distance between sluices (W) = 60 m

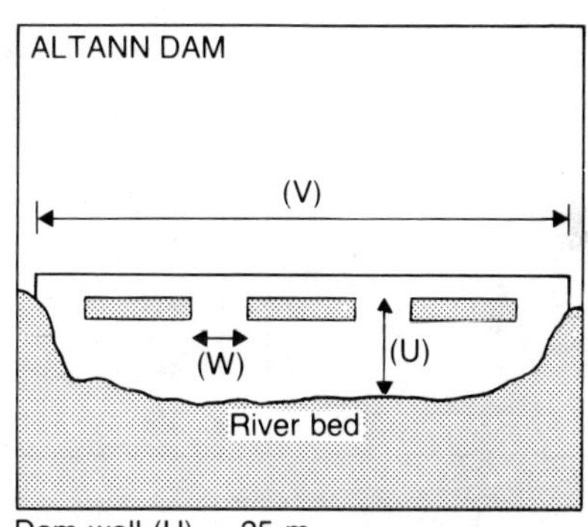

Dam wall (U) = 25 m
Dam width (V) = 1.8 km
Distance between sluices (W) = 300 m

Page 54

D1 This would now be a good follow-up exercise.
On the other hand, if the teacher has chosen not to use the supplementary exercises, **D1** provides a good opportunity for language focus.

If you establish that students are weaker at this than you had thought, go back and do the supplementary exercises after **D1**.

Page 54

D2/3 These lead up to report writing.
One of the central features of this report is comparison and contrast and the students will be required to make use of the grid that they have drawn up on the different energy sources. If you feel that students need more guidance before embarking on the writing, try this exercise.

Supplementary exercise

Ask students to note down answers to the following questions:

- Is your country agricultural or industrial?
- What is its population?
- Is the population evenly distributed, or are some areas more populated than others?
- What is most energy used for?
- Where is the main demand for energy?
- Are large or small scale schemes most appropriate?
- What natural resources are available?
- Is your country particularly suited to any of the energy sources discussed in terms of geographical location? (*e.g.* seismic area, lakes, rivers, coastal area, tidal estuaries, etc.)
- Does your country possess any major deposits of coal, oil or gas?
- What is the present major energy source?

Encourage students to consult the comparison grid when answering these questions in order to decide on the most suitable energy source for the future of their country.

Once individual students have made their decision, they should draw up a plan for their report.
The following could be suggested as a guideline.

Paragraph 1 State which energy source would be the most suitable.
Paragraph 2 Brief summary of geographical situation of country and reasons why this source is more suitable than others.
Paragraph 3 Outline of present energy demands/future needs.
Paragraph 4 Why other energy sources would be less suitable.

It should be made clear to students that the main reasons for doing this exercise are:

- to give them practice in using the language of comparison and contrast.
- to teach them to use notes effectively when writing.

When marking concentrate on these two points, and tell students that you will be doing this.
Ask them to hand in the grid they have been working on to ensure that they have taken account of the main points.

SECTION 3 — *SUMMARY*

In this section we take a closer look at a more conventional source of energy, nuclear energy, from various angles.

Students will:

- practise guessing the meaning of words from context.
- practise identifying attitudes in reading and listening.
- practise picking out main points from reading and listening.

- practise scanning text to find relevant information.
- practise making notes from reading.
- practise understanding the language of comparison and contrast in a listening exercise.
- practise taking notes from listening under main headings.
- practise writing a short passage using notes from listening and reading.
- practise using the language of comparison and contrast to write a short passage.

Teaching tips

Page 55

A1*a* The teacher can expect students to ask the following types of question:

- How expensive is nuclear power to produce?
- Is nuclear power more dangerous than other sources?
- What are the dangers of pollution from nuclear plants?
- How safe is it to work in/live near a nuclear plant?
- How does a nuclear reactor work?
- What fuel is necessary to produce nuclear power?
- Do we really need nuclear power?

When the students have drawn up their lists of questions with a partner, the teacher should conduct a feedback session and note the questions on the blackboard.

A1*b* The questions on the blackboard will act as a checklist for this scanning activity.

Page 55

A2*a*/*b* Ask students not to use a dictionary at this stage, but to rely on general knowledge and common sense.

Suggest that students draw up a table to note down their explanations. The table might look like this:

List of terms	Possible explanation	Further explanation from text
nuclear reactor	place where nuclear reaction takes place	part of power plant where nuclear reaction takes place and heat produced
uranium	radioactive material	radioactive * isotope
fission	?	splitting atoms to release energy
chain reaction	a series of reactions	continued process – reaction that keeps going on
moderator	something that makes a reaction more moderate	substance that slows down neutrons and makes them more efficient e.g. water, carbon

List of terms	Possible explanation	Further explanation from text
control rods	means of controlling reaction (poss. in reactor?)	absorb neutrons and slow down fission *e.g.* cadmium, boron
coolant	substance for cooling	used to remove heat to stop reactor melting *e.g.* air, CO_2, helium, water
turbine	part of generating equipment	is turned by steam, drives generator and produces electricity

If the teacher discovers that some students seem to have a better idea of nuclear power than others, have students swap partners a couple of times during this activity in order to share knowledge.

Page 55

A2*b* Students should note their improved explanations in the third column of the table.

Finally, students should be encouraged to use their dictionaries to look up any words that remain unclear and hinder their comprehension of the terms (*e.g.* * isotope).

Page 55

These three texts represent three very different perspectives on the topic of nuclear power.

The International Atomic Energy Agency is an organisation which promotes the development of nuclear power.

Greenpeace is an environmental group which is seriously concerned about nuclear power and on the whole opposes its development. Greenpeace encourages the development of alternative sources of energy.

G. Foley's book presents the facts on 'Energy' in a reasonably objective way and does not evidently take sides in the argument for or against nuclear power.

Page 58

B1/2 Students should be able to have a good guess at these attitudes just from the information in the references, as well as from the texts themselves.

If students have difficulty in distinguishing between the attitudes of the different authors, the following exercise might help.

Supplementary exercises

In this exercise questions 1–6 focus on the attitude of the author of Text 1, while questions 7–11 focus on Text 3.

1 The author of Text 1 maintains that supplies of wood, coal and oil are

a sufficient to meet world demand for energy.

b running out.

(Answer: *b* 'these sources decline . . . approach depletion')

2 The author of Text 1 believes that nuclear power is
a a conventional source of power.
b an alternative source of power.
(Answer: b 'other alternative energy sources')

3 The author of Text 1 feels that environmental questions
a should be considered when planning for energy production.
b are not important in the face of energy problems.
(Answer: *a* Paragraph 1)

4 The author of Text 1 believes that
a some environmental damage is necessary if we are to improve standards of living.
b no environmental damage is acceptable.
(Answer: *a* 'require that some environmental impact be accepted')

5 The author of Text 1 suggests that the nuclear industry
a takes account of environmental issues.
b ignores environmental issues.
(Answer: *a* 'nuclear industry has taken a leading role in addressing systematically both long and short term issues'

6 The author of Text 1
a warns against the development of nuclear power and its environmental consequences.
b reassures us that the nuclear industry is responsible.
(Answer: *b*)

7 The author of Text 3 seeks to assure us that the consequences of the Chernobyl accident were
a insignificant
b great.
(Answer: *b* see map)

8 The author of Text 3 compares Russian reactors with other European reactors to show
a that they are similar.
b that they are different.
(Answer: *a* 'like the Russian reactor . . . risk')

9 The author of Text 3 feels that the idea of estimating the number of accidents over 10,000 years is
a realistic
b unrealistic.
(Answer: *a* 'no reactor operates for 10,000 years')

10 The author of Text 3 believes that the possibility of another nuclear accident occurring soon
a is less than before Chernobyl.
b is the same as it always was.
(Answer: *b* 'could happen as easily tomorrow or the next day')

11 The author of Text 3
a warns us about some of the arguments used in decision-making.
b reassures us that the nuclear industry gives adequate consideration to public safety.
(Answer: *a* 'The notion of theoretical risk is an important decision-making and public relations tool . . .')

Page 58

C2*a* Encourage students to decide on the appropriate note form or combination of note forms to use here. They might consider using a flow chart (see Unit 1), outlining (this unit), key words (this unit) or a simplified diagram (adapting the one on page 56).

C2*b* Ask students to use a checklist, like the one on page 49, when comparing notes.

D2 Once this exercise has been completed, the teacher may wish to focus on some of the language of the interview. This could serve as a further step in preparing students for the note-making exercise in **D3** below.

Supplementary exercise

Write the following phrases on the board and ask students to listen to the interview again to decide whether these phrases are introducing a point of similarity (S) or a point of difference (D).

These phrases are underlined in the tapescript.

	Focus phrases	Answer
1	as opposed to	D
2	was of this type	S
3	but not of the same design	D
4	it's a different sort of	D
5	much more than	D
6	just as	S
7	much more slowly	D
8	both are thought to be	S
9	if you compare risks	D
10	is reckoned to be more economical	D
11	might turn out to be cheaper	D
12	either of these . . . will be cheaper	S

Page 58

D3 This exercise gives students the opportunity to consider how they are going to make their notes before they listen. Their job is made easier by the fact that the headings are provided, but students still have to decide what form the notes will take.

The teacher should therefore give the students an opportunity to make this decision and, if necessary, remind them of the four forms introduced to date: flow charts, outlining, key words, grids.

After they have completed the listening exercise, students should compare their notes

– to check for content and that important details have been noted.
– to discover which note form was most efficient.

A flow chart is not likely to be a suitable note form here, but any of the others would be acceptable if properly used. An example of grid notes for this exercise is provided in the key of the students' book.

Page 59

D4 This is a similar exercise to **D3** in Section 2. However, at this stage students should not need as much guidance.

The teacher could suggest that students use the text on page 48 and their answers to **D3** of Section 2 on page 54 as models.

The teacher should remind students of the necessity for a plan.

When correcting the students' work, the teacher should watch out for accurate use of the language of comparison and contrast.

The teacher might like to compare the errors that students make in this piece of work with those they made in previous work in this unit.

The work should be well paragraphed and students should be making use of markers such as:

As far as . . . is concerned
As regards
Turning now to
In terms of
With respect to

These markers appear in the model on page 48 of this unit.

SECTION 4 – *SUMMARY*

In this section students will have the opportunity to put into practice in a freer way the main skills that they will have learnt in this unit. All the information that they have gathered up to now on alternative power sources and on nuclear power will be of use to them.

Students will be engaged in:

– reading texts, maps and tables for specific information.
– making notes with a particular purpose in mind.
– arriving at a solution through comparison and contrast of various factors.
– discussing and planning strategies to achieve an aim.
– negotiating to reach a consensus or compromise.

Teaching tips

If you have been working through this book unit by unit, students will already have some experience of this type of freer fluency activity. To promote student independence and self-reliance, you could encourage them to take more responsibility for the running of the activity by asking them to decide on the number of roles and their allocation, and to select their own co-ordinator.

If students are slow to request meetings, the teacher or the co-ordinator should suggest who they might meet and discuss with. (See Co-ordinator's role, page 63 of the Students Book.)

The teacher should monitor the proceedings. This will involve sitting in on individual discussions, encouraging some measure of agreement between students, encouraging all students to get through the various stages in roughly the same time.

At the same time the teacher could take the opportunity to monitor the language used throughout the activity. Discrete notes of recurring mistakes would be valuable for later feedback, particularly concerning the language of comparison and contrast, but also in connection with appropriate language in meetings and discussions.

However, it is important that students should not feel that they are being closely observed for accuracy, since the main aim of the activity is fluency.

Pay attention to timing so that activities remain snappy. As a general rule, allow students a little less time than they really need for each activity, rather than too much.

The co-ordinator should interrupt discussions and ask students to move on to the next meeting if they tend to run over the time limit.

SECTION 5

Teaching tips

Page 64

A Writing subject notes

No doubt students will have their own styles of note-making for their subjects. This exercise can provide them with an opportunity to assess the effectiveness of these notes.

Ask students to bring examples of notes that they have taken in the past to your lesson.

Elicit a checklist of 'do's and don'ts' for note-making and put this on the blackboard.

Ask students to judge whether their own notes conform with the checklist.

Encourage students to swap their notes for a second opinion.

Suggest to students that they try a different system for subject notes.

Fix a day by which students will have tried a different system, and will bring these notes to class to assess them in a similar way.

B Coping with subject texts

Ask your students to carry out the tasks on subject texts as indicated in **B1–5**.

Agree on a date by which students will have completed the task.

On the appointed day, ask students to swap the texts they have read.

Have them indicate which sections they consider most important.

Have them ask their partners if they can locate the main points.

C Understanding subject talks

It is quite possible that some of your students do not normally need to take notes while listening on their present courses. However, it is likely that this will change in the future when students move on to other courses. Students having to take notes at lectures for the first time are often over-taxed in the early stages of their courses.

Some experience of this skill is therefore valuable.

Tell students that you wish them to take notes while listening to a teacher, tutor or lecturer at one lesson within a fixed amount of time.

Ask them to check the results against the checklist, **C1–4** on page 65.

Fix the target date for students to bring these listening notes to class.

Students might look at each other's notes and assess them.

D Writing Subject Passages

If you are able to liaise with subject teachers, this would be a good opportunity for joint preparation and joint marking of students' work.

TEST PRACTICE

Study Skills The questions which follow all refer to texts in Unit 3. In each case you should read quickly through the relevant text in order to answer the questions.

If you do these 40 questions as a test, they should take you no longer than an hour.

Part 1 – Solar energy *pages 50–51*

1 In the opening paragraphs the two headings (1 Direct Solar Technologies and 2 Biomass Energy) are
A two examples of uses of solar energy.
B two alternatives to solar energy.
C two types of solar energy to be dealt with in this article.
D two general ways of exploiting solar energy.

2 What is S.T.E.C.?
A an example of photovoltaics in use.
B a water heating system.
C a computer used to map the movement of the sun.
D an electricity generating plant in Japan.

3 The examples of countries where S.T.E.C. research has been done show that S.T.E.C.
A is already a world-wide and popular energy source.
B can be effective in any climate.
C is particularly suited to developing countries.
D has only been tried out in more developed countries.

4 What is the purpose of the paragraph entitled 'Photovoltaics – the principles' on page 50?
A To explain the scientific thinking behind the system.
B To outline the main advantages of this energy production system.
C To explain how to construct a photovoltaic system.
D To convince the reader of the practical nature of the system

5 What is the title of the paragraph which indicates the extent of the development of the S.T.E.C system?
A How it Works
B Future Prospects
C Present Schemes
D Pros and Cons

6 What is the aim of the paragraph entitled 'Costs and Investment' on page 51?
A To promote the S.T.E.C. system on the basis of low costs.
B To caution against the high costs of the S.T.E.C. system.
C To encourage more dependency on nuclear power.
D To promote photovoltaics for small communities.

7 How many advantages and disadvantages are mentioned in the final paragraph on page 51 (entitled 'Pros and Cons')?
A Three advantages and one disadvantage.

B Two advantages and two disadvantages.
C Two advantages and one disadvantage.
D One advantage and three disadvantages.

Part 2 – Solar and wind systems *page 51*

8 In general, this text
A outlines a number of technological advantages of solar energy.
B puts forward certain constraints concerning solar energy.
C weighs up the advantages and disadvantages of solar energy in terms of output.
D condemns solar energy as an impractical, expensive and overestimated power source.

9 What is the purpose of paragraph two of the text?
A It supports the main point of paragraph one.
B It defines solar energy.
C It contradicts the main point of paragraph one.
D It exemplifies a point made in paragraph one.

10 The third paragraph
A offers further arguments to support the ideas of paragraph two.
B puts arguments which are contradictory to those in paragraph one.
C develops one of the arguments presented in paragraph two.
D is not linked with what was said in paragraph one.

11 What is the writer's intention in the final paragraph?
A To suggest ways in which solar power can become economically viable.
B To describe a means of backing up solar power production.
C To compare solar, coal, oil and hydro power stations.
D To point out that solar power is not as reliable a source as hydro-electric power.

Part 3 – Geothermal power *pages 52–53*

12 Read the text and choose the correct series of labels for the diagram.
A 1 hot water
2 high temp.
3 hot water
4 turbine
B 1 cold water
2 hot rocks
3 hot water
4 turbine
C 1 reservoir
2 hot ground water
3 hot water
4 boiler
D 1 geyser
2 hot magma
3 hot water
4 geothermal reservoir

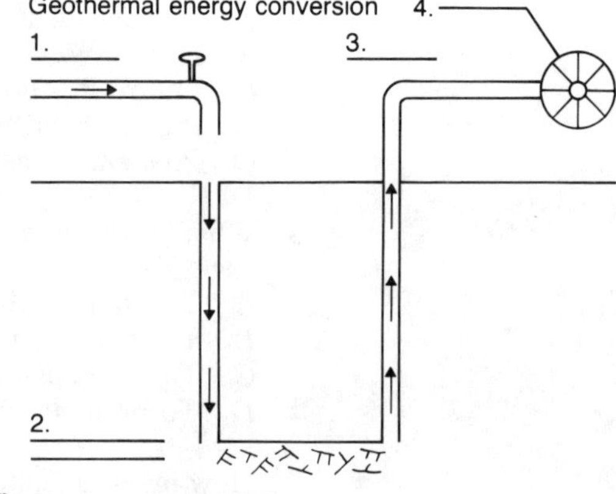

13 Which part of the text outlines a number of reasons why geothermal energy may not be the ideal energy source?

A Costs and Investments
B The Resource
C Pros and Cons
D Hot Dry Rocks

14 Seismic zones are
A areas of intensive earth heat
B areas where hot water flows.
C areas of the earth contaminated with radioactivity.
D the core of the earth.

15 Which of the following sentences best sums up the main point of the last paragraph on page 53?
A As far as costs are concerned, geothermal energy compares favourably with all other sources.
B Though not at all the cheapest small scale energy source, geothermal energy is the most economical large scale producer.
C Geothermal production is far more popular than all other known energy sources – except on a large scale.
D The development of geothermal energy holds promise for the future in terms of costs.

Part 4 – Environmental impacts of energy production *page 55*

16 The author of Text 1 believes
A that we could face an energy crisis.
B that no energy crisis is possible.
C that we have already avoided an energy crisis.
D that the world has already experienced an energy crisis.

17 The last sentence of paragraph two
A follows on directly from the points made up to that stage in the text.
B contrasts with an idea in paragraph two.
C contradicts the first sentence in the passage.
D is an example of a point made in paragraph two.

18 What is the writer's intention in paragraph three of this text?
A To promote a greater awareness of environmental issues.
B To explain in detail what kinds of environmental impact can be caused by energy production.
C To list the detrimental effects of nuclear power stations on our world.
D To assure us that effects on the environment are not ignored by the nuclear industry.

19 The word 'systematically' in the final line of this text suggests that
A the nuclear industry's attitude to the environment is a positive one.
B the nuclear industry's attitude to the environment is a negative one.
C the nuclear industry treats environmental problems in a haphazard way.
D the nuclear industry has no fixed policy on environmental issues, neither long term nor short term.

Part 5 – Nuclear energy *page 56*

20 In the first paragraph the author explains 'fission' as

A a radioactive isotope which occurs naturally.
B a substance which is closely related to uranium.
C a steady chain reaction.
D energy release as a result of splitting uranium-235 atoms.

21 The word 'Thus' in line 4 of paragraph two of this text
A indicates a contradiction of an idea stated previously.
B introduces an example of how the atom is split
C suggests an exception to the normal process of events.
D signals a further stage in the nuclear chain reaction.

22 In the first two sentences of paragraph three the author
A makes a distinction between nuclear power and nuclear weapons.
B issues a warning that nuclear bombs and nuclear reactors are closely related.
C points out a parallel between nuclear bombs and nuclear reactors.
D illustrates that nuclear and conventional power stations have nothing in common.

23 From the diagrams at the bottom of page 56 it can be seen that nuclear power stations differ from conventional power stations
A in their method of driving the turbine.
B in their method of generating electricity.
C in their method of heating the water.
D in their method of transmitting electricity.

24 The 'moderator' in paragraph four
A absorbs neutrons in order to slow them down.
B brings about fission by increasing the speed of moving neutrons.
C produces new neutrons by increasing the speed of fission.
D controls the speed of neutrons to ensure their efficiency.

25 Water' and 'carbon' in the last line of paragraph four of the text
A are two exceptions to moderators.
B are two possible examples of moderators.
C are the only examples of moderators.
D are two substitutes for moderators.

26 The second sentence in paragraph six 'Whether it is usefully used or not . .' tells us that
A heat is always removed.
B heat is usually removed.
C heat is sometimes removed.
D heat is never removed.

27 In paragraph six, carbon dioxide, helium and liquid sodium are
A examples of coolants used in one reactor type.
B examples of coolants used in two reactor types.
C examples of gases that can be used in reactors.
D examples of liquids that can be used in reactors.

28 In paragraph six we learn that
A there are two types of reactors, AGRs and PWRs.
B there are more than two types of reactors.

C the most common type of reactor is gas-cooled.
D most reactors use both liquid and gas as a coolant.

29 The author of this text
A would seem to agree with the author of the following text on the nuclear issue.
B would seem to disagree with the author of the following text on the nuclear issue.
C avoids moral issues concerning nuclear power.
D is mainly concerned with the moral issues raised by nuclear power.

Part 6 – Theoretical risk *page 57*

30 The author of this text maintains that calculation of the theoretical risk of a nuclear disaster
A is a useful guideline for assessing risk.
B is a means of giving people a sense of security.
C is a guarantee that nothing will ever happen.
D is a precise and accurate mathematical formula.

31 The author compares 'Russian reactors' with other European reactors
A to show that they are equally dangerous.
B to demonstrate that they have similar dimensions.
C to suggest that an accident on the same scale as Chernobyl could not happen in Western Europe.
D to argue that 'Russian' reactors are inferior to reactors elsewhere in the world.

Part 7 – Index

Refer to the following extract of an index from W.C. Patterson, *Nuclear Power*. Pelican, 1983.

32 How many pages are referred to under the entry for AGRs?
A more than five
B six
C five
D less than five

33 If you were looking for information on organisation set up to safeguard a population against the possibility of nuclear war, which page would you refer to?
A 128
B 106
C 215
D 117

34 Which of the following references share the same pagination?
A Argentina and Australia
B 'Able' test and APS-1
C Atomic Industrial Forum and AGRs
D 'Atoms for Peace' and Atomic Energy Act

Part 8 – Contents page

Refer to the following extract taken from W.C. Patterson, *Nuclear Power*. Pelican, 1983.

35 Which pages would you turn to if you wanted a definition of the term 'nuclear fusion'?
A 21
B 177
C 220
D 237

36 If you wanted to find out if the book contained a diagram of an Advanced Gas-cooled Reactor, which page would you turn to first?
A 9
B 23
C 40
D 220

37 Which chapter would you look at for information on the costs of nuclear energy production?
A 5
B 6
C 7
D 8

Contents

General Questions

For these questions you will need to look again through the texts on pages 50–54 and 55–57 of Unit 3.

38 Which of the texts in Unit 3 of the Students' Book are organised in a similar way?

A 'Solar Energy' on page 50 and 'Nuclear Energy' on page 56.
B 'Environmental Impacts of Energy Production' on page 55 and 'Theoretical Risk' on page 57.
C 'Power from Hot Rocks and Warm Water' on page 53 and 'Earth' on page 54.
D 'Solar Energy' on page 50 and 'Geothermal Power' on page 52.

39 Which of the texts below is the least subjective?

A 'Solar Energy' on page 50.
B 'Nuclear Energy' on page 56.
C 'Earth' on page 54.
D 'Theoretical Risk' on page 57.

40 Which of the texts listed below would be the most useful source of information if you were writing an essay on 'Economic considerations and energy policy'?

A 'Environmental Impacts on Energy Production' on page 55.
B 'Power from Hot Rocks and Warm Water' on page 53.
C 'Geothermal Power' on page 52.
D 'Earth' on page 54.

UNIT 4 · *Ringing the changes*

INTRODUCTION

This Unit is concerned with various aspects of our environment and some of the developments it is undergoing. The students' own personal experience of change is called into play and from there the Unit endeavours to explore the broader implications of ecological change.
In this Unit the students are introduced to 'mind maps', perhaps for the first time. This will increase their repertoire of note-making styles, and introduce an important revision strategy.

OBJECTIVES OF THIS UNIT

Here we are mainly concerned with three things.

1 Teaching students to pick out and use the language, vocabulary and grammar necessary to describe change and development, graphs and charts.
2 Teaching students further note-making strategies, namely mind maps.
3 Teaching students to use a body of texts and information in order to prepare and assess talks on a given topic.

SECTION 1 – *SUMMARY*

In this section students will:

- practise talking in continuous blocks to describe changes.
- practise listening to interviews to understand general meaning.
- practise listening for precise details.
- learn to listen for the attitude of speakers.
- learn the language necessary for describing recent change.
- practise the use of the present perfect tense in talking about change.
- learn to write a short passage to describe a place.

The questions and quote on page 67 serve to get the students thinking and talking about change in a variety of contexts. By having the students think about this in personal terms

- they are introduced to the concept which is central to the whole unit.
- they will employ the target language in a natural way.

Teaching tips

Page 66

A1 The teacher should monitor the language that the students are using to describe changes and check if there are any major difficulties here.

Students will probably need to use the present perfect, the simple past and the simple present verb forms.

If students are having problems with tenses here, there is no need for the teacher to focus on it yet. An opportunity for this will arise on page 68 in exercise **C**.

Page 67

A2 To discover the class's attitude to change, the teacher could ask the following questions.

- What are the most common areas of change that students have noticed?
- What particular changes do most people welcome?
- What changes are least welcome?
- What does the class feel is the most common reason for change in our world?
- Is our world developing at the same rate as in the past?

Page 67

B1 Students will need a few minutes to consider these questions and make their own notes on them.

If students come from the same country or area, try putting them in pairs or small groups to discuss these questions.

B2 If students have been working in pairs or groups, make sure that they swap for this activity.

The teacher should sit in on the exchanges. This is another opportunity for the teacher to monitor the language of change. Students will also be talking about predictions for the future. The teacher could therefore listen for the use of the language of prediction, such as 'will', 'might', 'may', 'could', 'perhaps' etc.

Page 68

C As an introduction to this activity, ask students if they know anything about Malacca, for example:

- where it is?
- what it is famous for?

C1 When students are considering the questions before they listen, encourage them to speculate about what the answers might be.

Note the guesses on the blackboard as a checklist.

Page 68

C2 If students have difficulty in noting what the speakers say about these topics, play the relevant clips again.

This exercise should provide the teacher with an opportunity to focus on the uses of the present perfect to describe recent changes.

Should students have any difficulty in understanding this concept, the teacher could illustrate the point with a time line, as in the exercise below.

Supplementary exercise

A time line shows in graphic form when an event occurred.

- If the event happened at a particular point in time, it is usually expressed in a past tense.

We indicate this on our time line with an X, and if it lasted a precise length of time, we mark this with two Xs.

– If, on the other hand, an event occurred in the past, but continues to have a direct effect on the present, we use the present perfect form. We indicate this on our time line with a spot to mark the point when it started, and a bracket to extend it into the present.

Copy the time line below on the blackboard, leaving it blank, and explain its meaning to the students.

Now write the two example sentences, *a* and *b*, on the blackboard, and mark the events on the time line.

a Malacca was founded somewhere between 1382 and 1411.
b Malacca has been a state since 1957.

Ask students to mark the following details on the time line in an appropriate way.

c The Japanese invaded Malacca in 1941.
d The town has been in existence for around 600 years.
e The population has greatly increased since 1818, when it was only 12,706.
f The Dutch conquered Malacca in about 1511 and remained there for 130 years.
g In 1641 the Portuguese first arrived in the town, and their influence has remained to the present day.
h The British occupied Malacca in 1795.
i The importance of Malacca as a port has greatly dwindled over the past century or so.
j Malaysia (and Malacca) have been independent since 1957.

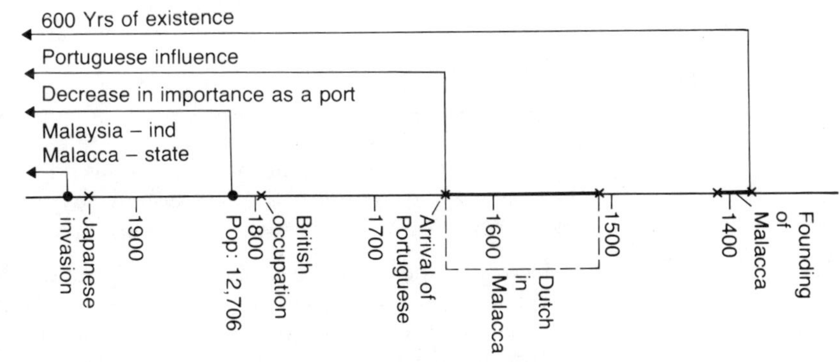

Ask the students to read back the details from their time line in a full class feedback.

Pay attention to the correct use of the present perfect and past tenses.

D This writing exercise could be given as homework. It is an important part of this section, as it permits students to employ the concepts and language they have met so far in this unit.

Encourage students to use some of the expressions they noted down in **C2**.

When correcting, pay special attention to correct verb forms and correct use of any vocabulary that has just arisen.

SECTION 2 – *SUMMARY*

In this section students will:

– practise talking about change with reference to the environment.
– practise scanning text for particular information.
– practise picking out the overall function of a text, a graph or a chart.
– practise identifying the main points of a text.
– learn how to use mind maps as a note-making technique.
– learn the language necessary for describing and interpreting trends and predictions.
– learn to write short passages to describe, interpret and make predictions about tabulated data, such as charts, graphs and pie charts.

Having considered change in a broad sense, students will now look at environmental change and its consequences.

In this section, and section 3, we introduce students to issues which are widely discussed today and are of interest to most people around the world.

It is worth pointing out that the general point of view of these texts is an 'environmentalist' one, and as the teacher or students may not entirely agree with the views expressed, there is plenty of scope for discussion.

Teaching tips

Page 69

A Students who are not familiar with the environmentalist cause may need an introduction to the topic. The following warm-up exercise may be useful for this.

Supplementary exercise

What is an 'ecosystem'?

Before students look at the cartoon on this page, ask them to consider the title of the section, The Ecosystem, by working through these questions.

– How can the word be broken up? (Eco/system)
– What other words contain the prefix 'eco'? (economy, ecology . . .)
– What do you think the prefix 'eco' could mean? (. . . in composition/concerned with habitat and environment)
– Look up the word 'ecosystem' in a dictionary. (e.g. Chambers: 'a unit consisting of a community of organisms and their environment')
– Compare the dictionary definition with the one at the top of page 69 in the Students' Book.
– Decide which of the two definitions is more biased towards the idea of 'preserving the ecosystem'. (The definition on page 69 is clearly an 'environmentalist' one.)

The meaning of this cartoon may not be immediately evident to students not familiar with the environmentalist way of thinking.
If the teacher wishes the students to get a better understanding of the implications, elicit some information with the following questions:

- What do we mean by 'natural resources'?
- What do we use them for?
- How do humans affect the ecosystem?
- Is the term 'chauvinist' a positive or a negative one?

Page 69

A1 Ask the students if they know of other uses of the word 'chauvinist'. (national chauvinism = extravagant pride in one's country with a contempt for foreign nations. male chauvinism = arrogance on the part of men towards women)

Have the students check the meaning of chauvinist in the dictionary.

Page 70

A3 In a feedback on this exercise the teacher should ask the group for a list of 'threats' and put these on the blackboard. Students may suggest some of the following:

water and air pollution/over-fishing/poaching/destroying forests/use of pesticides and herbicides, etc.

Page 71

B2 After completing this exercise, students will be aware that the text on page 70 is concerned with various threats to arable land and their causes. It contains a wealth of information which could prove valuable for the simulation in Section 4.

Supplementary exercise

If the teacher wishes to focus the students' attention further on this information, and at the same time give a deeper insight into the organisation of the text, the following exercise should help.

Find the terms in the text which mean the following:

1. land fit for ploughing and tillage (arable land)
2. the wearing away of earth (soil erosion)
3. nourishing elements in the earth (nutrients)
4. concentrated use of the land (intensive farming)
5. increasing the amount of food grown per acre (intensifying production)
6. the state of being dry and unproductive (aridity)
7. to grow worse (deteriorate)
8. cultivating the land too much (overcropping)
9. allowing animals to trample and eat down vegetation (overgrazing)
10. salt contamination of the soil (salinization)
11. an increase in atmospheric temperature due to an increase in carbon dioxide in the air (the greenhouse effect)
12. the action of chopping down trees (felling)

Page 71

B3 Having completed this exercise the teacher may still feel that students have difficulties in transferring the information to the mind map. This may be an indication that students have not come to grips with the relationship of cause and effect, so important throughout the text on page 70.

The following series of tasks should help to make this more explicit.

Supplementary exercise

Look at your mind map and the text, and decide which phrase in each of the pairs below expresses **cause**, and which one expresses **effect**.

1	use of intensive methods of farming (C)	loss of organic matter in the topsoil (E)
2	desertification (E)	overcropping (C)
3	desertification (E)	deforestation (C)
4	deforestation (C)	soil erosion (E)
5	climatic change (E)	the greenhouse effect (C)
6	exposing thin tropical soils to the elements (C)	their eventual disappearance (E)
7	agriculture (C)	felling (E)
8	scarcity of timber (C)	fuel-wood problems (E)

(The answers are given in brackets C= cause E= effect)

Note down the phrases in the text which helped you to decide on your answers.

(Answers: **1** is leading to **2** is being produced by **3** can also be produced by **4** results in **5** occurs as a result of **6** often leads to **7** is still the commonest reason for **8** is leading to)

Page 72

B4 Having completed this exercise, the students could be asked to examine the seven sentences again and pick out the phrases which indicate the relationship between cause and effect.

Supplementary exercise

To practise the language and vocabulary that has been activated in this section so far, the teacher might now ask students to write a short summary describing 'Threats to arable land'.

Pages 72–76

C Here students are introduced to and given the opportunity to practise the language of trends.

C3*d* This exercise offers students a standard plan for describing, interpreting and predicting.

The teacher might like to draw students' attention to the organisation of this passage, and encourage them to follow a similar pattern in exercise **D**.

SECTION 3 – *SUMMARY*

In this section students will:

- practise listening to an interview to identify the main points and take notes.
- practise summarising notes in mind map form.

- learn to identify predictions made by a speaker and decide on their degree of certainty.
- practice predicting the content of a text from its title.
- practise identifying similarity and difference in a text and summarising this information in chart and passage form.
- practise putting their own views in a discussion.
- learn to prepare, give and assess a short talk.

This section is of relevance to the role play in Section 4, as it provides further useful information and ideas on ecological change.

Topics that have arisen in previous sections, such as the greenhouse effect, deforestation and reduction in genetic variation are elaborated on here. The last of these is also valuable background information for Unit 6, A Brave New World.

Teaching tips

Page 76

A1*a* Allow only a few minutes for this exercise and then gather ideas from the class for a blackboard checklist.

Students might suggest some of the products and their possible effects, as listed below:

Products	**Effects**
exhaust fumes factory emissions	carbon dioxide increase → greenhouse effect → climatic change
coal power station emissions	sulphur dioxide increase → acid rain
aerosols	ozone layer problems
chemical sprays e.g. pesticides herbicides	pollution of land, air and water
burning of plastics	air pollution → cancer?

Page 76

A1*b* Encourage students to use a chart similar to the one above to record the speaker's answers.

A4*b* The teacher does not need to replay the whole interview for this exercise. The relevant extracts have been recorded separately, after the interview.

A4*c* The teacher could ask students to order the five extracts according to how definite the speaker is in each case. The students might suggest this order: **1**/**3**/**2**/**4**/**5**. However, it is difficult to say whether **1** or **3** is more definite, and this could be discussed.

The teacher could point out that:

- 'will' is more definite than 'might'.
- the addition of 'I think' and 'almost' to **2** makes the sentence more tentative.

The teacher could discuss with the class whether the speaker is less sure of his facts in **2**, or whether he is simply being polite.

Extracts

1 And without question by the end of this century we will cross the 600 mark.
2 I think it's almost inevitable that we will move the climate system outside the natural range.
3 There will assuredly be winners and losers in the question of global climate change.
4 Our best guess would be that countries in the far north will, on the whole, benefit.
5 But countries that are reasonably well off today might suffer.

Page 78

B2 The students now attempt a mind map alone and the teacher may decide to provide some extra guidance.

Make sure students decide on a suitable short heading.

Make sure this heading goes to the centre of the page and that it stands out visually.

Remind students to start at the top of the map (at 1 o'clock) and to work clockwise.

Encourage students to make sure their map has visual impact.

Supplementary exercise

The text on page 77 contains a number of words that can be used in a variety of contexts. This exercise asks students:

- firstly, to examine some of these words in the context of this text to discover their meaning here.
- and secondly, to use their prior knowledge, the knowledge of their fellow students and dictionaries, to get a better idea of the range of meanings that these words can have in other contexts.

Below is a list of possible focus words. The teacher should amend this list according to the time available for this exercise and the vocabulary level of the students.

Put the list on the blackboard:

supports	adapted	emerge	cultivate
recorded	extracted	developed	resistant
saved	to fall back on		grafting

Have the students draw up a chart similar to the one below, and note down the phrases in which the words occur in this text.

Focus words	Phrase in context	Other possible contexts
supports	the earth supports many species	– He supports Liverpool football club. – The column supports the roof. – The daughter supports her old mother.

(An example, supports, has already been completed.)

Now ask students to think of other contexts in which these words could be used, and to note down phrases or sentences to illustrate this.
Ask students to compare their findings and, if necessary, to check their answers in a dictionary.

Page 78

C1*a* Encourage students to examine the two words of the title for clues to the meaning of **Biosphere reserves.**

- Ask students to break the words up into 'meaning blocks'. (bio sphere reserves)
- Ask students what other words they associate with:
  bio (biology, biochemistry, biotechnology ...)
  sphere (hemisphere, atmosphere, spherical, ...)
  reserve (nature reserve, reserve a table, a reserved person ...)
- Ask students to look up the meaning of these words and word parts in a dictionary:
  bio (living organisms ...)
  biosphere (the part of the earth and its atmosphere in which living things are found)
  reserve (land reserved for a special purpose ...)

Supplementary exercise

The text, Biosphere Reserves, contains a lot of environmentalist terminology, and a pre-reading vocabulary exercise would serve to make the text more accessible to students. This should be done before exercise **C1***b*, *i.e* before the students read the text.

The teacher should put this list of words from the first two paragraphs of the text on the blackboard:

flora and fauna
genetic diversity
ecological area
research
uninhabited
conservation
human interference

Tell the students that they are going to read a text in which these words appear.
Ask students, in groups, to speculate further on the meaning of Biosphere Reserves and to predict more precisely what the text is going to be about.

Page 78

C1*b* Ask students to check their understanding of the meaning of Biosphere Reserves by reading the text.

Page 78

C2*a* Ask students to consider what types of note form they could use here. (*e.g.* diagram, mind map, chart, outlining)
Ask the different groups to choose one of these note forms to present their notes.

Page 78

C2*b* Once the students have completed this note-taking task, pass the different sets of notes around the class, and discuss the advantages and the disadvantages of each.

Page 79

D This activity could provide practice of formal discussion techniques.

Divide the class into groups of no less than four students.

Tell each group to appoint a chairperson, who will lead the group and note the opinions of the members on each of the three discussion points.

Point out that the students do not have to reach a consensus in their group discussions. The chairperson can report split opinions.

Agree on a limited time for the discussion and inform the chairpersons that they will report back on opinions expressed.

The teacher can take the opportunity of monitoring these discussions, by sitting on the edge of each group and discretely making notes.
Notes on good meeting practice, constant errors in meeting conduct and recurring language errors could provide the basis for valuable feedback at the end of the session.

Page 79

E The final activity of the section is concerned with preparing students to give short, well organised talks to a group. Many activities throughout this book depend on students' ability to make presentations to groups. This is a useful skill in many academic and professional areas.

E2/3 Limit the students' time for these activities since these are tasks they should be able to perform rapidly.

Encourage students to use the notes they have already made throughout the Unit and to refer back to the texts for further information.

E4 Once students have drawn up their final plan, ask them to check their language by referring to the table in the key.

Page 80

E5 The assessment chart might have as its main headings those listed on page 80, under Notes on Delivery.
The chart might look like this:

Assessment chart for talks

	very good	fair	needs improvement	comment
Stance	√			
Voice			√	Too low
Pace		√		Could be faster
Audience Contact			√	Eyes down/no eye contact
Timing			√	Spoke for 5 minutes

SECTION 4 – *SUMMARY*

Once students have reached this stage in the Unit, they will have gathered a reasonable amount of information and details concerning the environment and ecosystems. This section provides students with the opportunity to reorganise this knowledge and make use of it.

Students are presented with a problem and required to adopt and defend a point of view. This involves conducting investigations, collating information and presenting a case.

In this section students will:

- practise reading longer texts for specific information.
- practise identifying the 'angle' of a text on a particular subject.
- practise picking out and noting main points in a suitable note form.
- practise referring to texts for information to prepare a presentation.
- practise delivering a presentation to a group.
- practise participating in a discussion.
- practise writing a report from a given angle.

Teaching tips

Pages 81–85

There is little doubt that the three texts presented here take an environmentalist stance on the rainforest issue.

But just how do they get their message across?

Is it stated frankly within the text?

A subtle and effective way of getting a message across is to transmit it through choice of language. Adverts are a good example of this.

The following exercise provides the teacher with an opportunity to focus on this and to examine more closely the language of these texts.

Supplementary exercise

The phrases and sentences below are taken from the first three paragraphs of Text 1, 'What makes rainforests so special?'

Put this blank chart on the blackboard and ask students to copy it.

Write in the focus phrases in the left column.

Complete the exercise for the first phrase, 'by far the most diverse', by indicating that this has positive connotations and by suggesting a more neutral alternative.

Ask students to complete the chart for the other focus phrases. (Suggested answers have been included here for the teacher's convenience.)

	Connotations		
Focus phrases	**Negative**	**Positive**	**Neutral alternative**
... tropical forests are by far the most diverse ...		√	contain more species than other ecosystems

Focus phrases	Connotations: Negative	Connotations: Positive	Neutral alternative
. . . precious reservoirs of animals and plants . . .		√	areas containing many animals and plants
. . . are being destroyed at an appalling rate . . .	√		are being cut down rapidly
. . . forest will disappear . . .	√		forest will be cleared
. . . the immense extinction of plant and animal species . . .	√		the reduction in the number of species
. . . so rich in species . . .		√	contain so many species
. . . what will necessarily become mere fragments of the Earth's former forests . . .	√		the existing forests

Now ask students to read Text 3, 'Every year 11 million acres . . .', on page 85 and to note down words or phrases that might bias the reader.

Ask students to think of and note down phrases which are less biased. This text is rich in such language. Here are some phrases and more neutral alternatives that students might suggest:

Phrases in text	Neutral alternatives
rainforests are destroyed for the sake of convenience	forests are cut down to supply people's needs
contributes to this destruction	results in felling
nearly half of all rain-forests have been wiped out	large areas of rainforest have been cut down
with them went countless unique and exotic wild creatures	species were made extinct
native peoples have been driven from their home-lands, often into poverty and famine	people have been displaced
weather patterns the world over are being upset	the climate is being changed
the absurd thing is it doesn't have to happen	it is unnecessary

Page 85

B1 This activity mainly refers to Text 2, 'Rainforests face attack of double standards.'

In order to answer the questions in this exercise, students will probably need to scan the text again.

B2 The instructions for the organisation of the public enquiry have deliberately been left open to encourage students to make some decisions for themselves.

Page 86

B4 During the enquiry the teacher might monitor the following:

- **Effective presentations** In order to do this the teacher could use a checklist similar to the ones students have drawn up.

  At the end of the activity the teacher could make general comments on strengths and weaknesses of the class's performance.

  Alternatively, the teacher could make brief notes on each presentation, and hand these to the groups at the end.
- **Discussion strategies** Here too the strengths and weaknesses of the participants could be noted by the teacher. In particular the teacher might pay attention to methods used for interrupting, making a point, agreeing and disagreeing with other speakers.

  In a feedback at the end, the teacher could highlight good strategies employed by students, and discuss improvements to weaker strategies.

It is important that feedback by the teacher is not all negative. This discussion will have been a complex task for many students and it is vital for future motivation that they feel that they have been successful to some degree.

Page 86

C Clearly, the type of report that students write as a result of the enquiry will vary according to which publication it is written for.

Students should be encouraged to discuss what angle these various publications might take on the issue.

Students should then decide which one they personally want to write for. They should be encouraged to throw themselves into the task whole-heartedly and try to adopt the point of view of the publication.

The teacher could have the students plan their reports in groups, where they should be encouraged to consider the factors which will influence what they write. This will involve considering the type of language that they use and its connotations. Also important will be the points they choose to stress and, indeed, the points they choose to leave out.

The measure of success of these articles will not depend on the level of accuracy of the language used. Instead, the teacher should look for effectiveness in conveying the 'angle' of the publication.

SECTION 5

Page 86

A Mind maps

Students who have not used this note-making technique before may be reluctant to try it out.

It is the authors' experience that many students tend not to take it seriously initially and are reluctant to try it out. It is therefore necessary that the teacher persists and encourages students to attempt it at least once on their own.

It is also the authors' experience that after the initial attempts, many students adopt the technique enthusiastically; personalise it and develop their own particular style. Consequently, there will probably be great variation of mind map styles within the class.

Students may find it easier to start off by using mind maps in order to reorganise existing reading and listening notes. Indeed, this is an excellent technique for getting students to revise their subject notes. The teacher should stress the use of mind maps as a revision technique, and the fact that their visual nature facilitates memorising.

Supplementary exercise

To demonstrate that mind maps make information easy to memorise, try the following exercise.

Divide the class into two groups.

Ask one group to look at the linear notes in the box on page 87, and to cover the mind map which follows them.

Ask the other group to look at the mind map on page 87 and cover the boxed linear notes.

Set a time limit of no more than 2 minutes and instruct students to study the notes.

Tell all students to close their book and ask them, working alone, to write down as much information as they can remember in 2 to 3 minutes.

Ask students to compare their results.

There is no proof that students working from mind maps always remember more, but they may:

- retain the organisation better.
- remember the information for longer.
- remember more key words.

B Reading texts

There is no doubt that on most courses one of the most difficult things that students have to do is deal with vast amounts of reading. Students often tend to see subject textbooks as impenetrable without subject teacher guidance. The ability to preview a text is one way students might find their own path through the forest of material, and learn to be selective in what they read.

TEST PRACTICE

Writing

Question 1

Choose **one** of the following note-taking exercises.

a Refer to the text on page 70 in Unit 4.
By means of a table show the various threats to arable land and their causes.

b Refer to the text 'Rainforests face attack of double standards' on page 83 in Unit 4.
In flowchart form show how Hawaii has developed since the fifth century.

c Using information from any of the texts in Unit 4, make notes in any appropriate form to show the advantages of preserving rainforests.

Question 2

You must choose **one** of the titles below and write at least 60 of your own words. Do not copy sentences from the text.

a The texts on pages 77 and 78 in Unit 4 stress the importance of saving as many species as possible from extinction.
Do you feel that this is an important issue? Discuss the relevance of these ideas to your own country.

b In spite of opposition, rainforests continue to be destroyed. A number of possible reasons for this are given in the texts in Unit 4.
In your opinion, what are the principal reasons that explain the continued destruction of the rainforests?

b One possible version of this flow chart could look like this:

Flow-chart to show development of Hawaii since 15th century

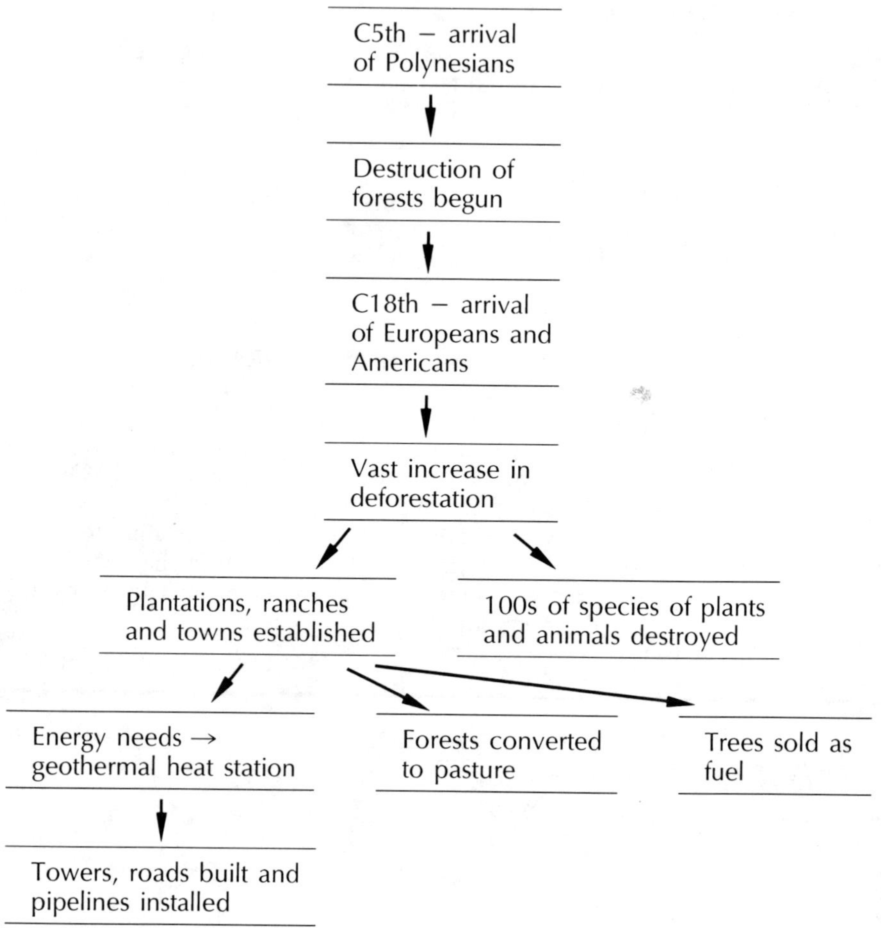

UNIT 5 · *Food for thought*

INTRODUCTION

Everybody likes to talk about home. This Unit gives students the opportunity to talk about various aspects of their home environment.

Here, students will discuss the way of life that they are familiar with and features of it, such as food, agriculture and fisheries.

This will culminate in the Test Practice section, where students will practise talking about where they come from in an interesting way. The object of this is to improve their interview skills.

OBJECTIVES OF THIS UNIT

Here we are mainly concerned with two things:

1 Teaching students to give clear and persuasive explanations in written and spoken form.

2 Teaching students to cope with unfamiliar words by using all of the available clues in the text.

SECTION 1 – *SUMMARY*

In this section students will:

- practise predicting text content from a title.
- practise scanning text to check predictions about content.
- learn to make outline notes from a text.

Teaching tips

Page 89

A The teacher should monitor the language that the students are using to list the reasons. Students will probably need to make use of the active and passive voice in the simple present tense to list the factors accurately.

Page 89

A2 If the students have difficulty in predicting the possible meaning the following multiple-choice question may help direct their reading.

Do you think the article will describe

A an attempt to grow more food?
B an attempt to export more food?
C an attempt to import more food?
D an attempt to distribute food more fairly?

Supplementary exercise

A good way of giving students extra practice in this skill is by:

1 distributing the headlines of newspaper articles or titles of magazine articles;

2 allowing the students a few minutes to predict the likely content of the articles;

3 distributing copies of the articles themselves so that the students can see if their predictions were correct.

Students can practise this skill in their own time using texts from their subject specialisms as well as articles of general interest.

Page 91

B1 In making their evaluation of the notes students should be actively encouraged to refer back to the contents of the original article. This will enable them to check whether the main points have been included and also see on what basis others were left out.

With regard to the actual presentation of the information, some students may benefit from actually reconstituting it in another form rather than simply talking about it.

Working alone each student should present the information using a format they think is simple to record and easy to recall.

They should then exchange their notes with fellow students who can evaluate them according to the criteria in *B1 a – f.*

Supplementary exercise

Often students who can understand the meaning of a set of words may need practice in understanding how a writer makes use of them to express his meaning. This exercise should help them be more aware of how a writer does this. Refer to the article on page 90.

1 What is the writer's intention in the first paragraph?
A To criticise the agricultural policies of most African countries.
B To account for the failure of most African countries policies.
C To suggest that an alternative policy has been successful.
D To suggest that workable alternatives exist.

2 The 'other face of African agriculture' (paragraph 2)
A illustrates the problem contained in paragraph 1.
B exaggerates the problem contained in paragraph 1.
C solves the problem contained in paragraph 1.
D underlines the problems contained in paragraph 1.

3 What is the purpose of the fifth paragraph in the second column which begins 'Nowhere is this . . . .'?
A It introduces a description of the point made in the previous paragraph.
B It introduces an example of the point made in the previous paragraph.
C It introduces an analysis of the point made in the previous paragraph.

D It introduces an alternative to the point made in the previous paragraph.

4 According to the writer, how significant were natural resources in explaining Cameroon's success?
A Self-sufficiency in food production is determined by the optimum utilization of natural resources.
B Natural resources were the determining factor in achieving self-sufficiency in food production.
C Self-sufficiency in food production is not only determined by the availability of natural resources.
D Self-sufficiency in food production is determined by the exploitation of natural resources.

5 The relationship between 'food production' and 'illiteracy' in this case demonstrates that
A food production is unaffected by a rise in the level of literacy.
B rising literacy affects the level of food production.
C rising literacy is one of the effects of increased food production.
D literacy is unaffected by a rise in the level of food production.

6 The writer's example of the NW province illustrates his point that
A natural disasters bring increased foreign aid.
B the farmers must accept the latest methods without question.
C the latest methods must be made practical and adapted to the farms.
D the latest methods are practically the only way to significantly increase food production.

7 In this article the writer demonstrates that
A price controls are more effective than subsidies.
B subsidies are more effective than price controls.
C subsidies are more effective than incentives.
D incentives are more effective than subsidies.

Answers: **1***C* **2***C* **3***B* **4***C* **5***C* **6***C* **7***D*

Page 91

B2 Students should be made aware that they must now turn their attention to the whole text and not just the first part of it.

To avoid a passive answer to the question of whether the main points have been included, students should be encouraged to reread the main article actively and see whether any major points have been left out.

Some of the missing points the students may find are:

- The causes of self-sufficiency in the NW province.
- The importance of research and development.
- The disincentives given to producers of export crops.

With regard to the format of the notes, students should again be referred back to the criteria on the previous page in order to make an accurate evaluation.

SECTION 2 — *SUMMARY*

In this section students will:

- practise making notes while listening.
- learn to make explanations using the language of cause and effect.
- practise using notes to present ideas visually to an audience.
- learn to speak persuasively, taking into account the attitudes and knowledge of the audience.

Teaching tips

A2 *Page 92*

Supplementary exercise

If the students have difficulty identifying the phrases of explanation used by the speaker ask them to identify them from the following list:

because of	owing to
thereby	as a result of
caused by	therefore
in consequence	in order to
due to	caused you to

In order to help them understand the exact meanings of these phrases in context, give them the following questions.

Select why the speakers on the tape use the following expressions:

1 because of
A To indicate the relationship between price and planning.
B To explain the relationship between GDP and exports.
C To account for the variation in export earnings.
D To account for variations in cocoa production.

2 due to
A To explain the relationship between crop production and price.
B To explain variations in price.
C To explain government incentives to grow other crops.
D To explain the relationship between price and consumer demand.

3 owing to
A To explain how the Cameroons earn foreign currency.
B To explain why the Cameroons need foreign currency.
C To explain the effect of the self-sufficiency policy.
D To demonstrate the importance of foreign currency earnings.

4 as a result of
A To explain why the Cameroons do not need outside help.

B To indicate the reasons for outside help.
C To show the sole source of outside help.
D To explain the independent role of IFAD.

Answers: **1***A* **2***A* **3***C* **4***A*

Page 92

A3 Before students begin this task they should be encouraged to decide what factors cause people to have persuasive ability. They should then formulate criteria which will enable group members to evaluate objectively the performance of the 'Ministry official' in their group.

Among the factors students may mention in determining their criteria of persuasiveness are:

- presentation of argument
- clear organisation of argument
- ability to see the other persons point of view and deal with any fears or uncertainties
- ability to remain calm under pressure
- ability to vary the technique of explanation avoiding undue repetition
- to summarise the main points comprehensively

It should be pointed out to the students that the words and phrases recorded in **A2** could be usefully employed in their follow-up discussion about the 'Ministers' performances.

Page 92

B It is important to remind students that they must not only use their note-taking technique to remember the information they are going to present, they must also use it to help the audience understand. Students should be encouraged to construct the set of notes on the blackboard as they talk without facing the blackboard.

B2 Before beginning this task students may compare the likely attitudes and behaviour of the two groups and what they will expect from the speaker and note the type of language to be used in each case.

Whilst the speeches are being delivered the rest of the class should adopt seating or standing arrangements which try to create an atmosphere something like the two situations. They should also be encouraged to behave in a relevant manner and ask questions which are relevant to the particular situation.

Supplementary exercise

Weaker students may gain some idea of the appropriacy of language by deciding which of the two speeches the following extracts are taken from.

	Answers
The distribution of the catch to the wholesaler is normally carried out at once.	*(ii)*
Thereafter the product is packed in ice prior to its distribution to retail outlets.	*(ii)*
How often do you have enough to feed you and your family during the rainy season?	*(i)*

Owing to the seasonal variations in income due to climatic factors fishermen are rarely able to enjoy a stable level of income.	*(ii)*
Think of the hours your wives and daughters have had to toil in the hot sun just so that you have enough to feed the little ones.	*(i)*
Other members of the family are often required to supplement the family income by engaging in activities such as shellfish collection at low tide.	*(ii)*
The government is doing everything in its power to ensure that all fishermen will enjoy a higher level of income in the future.	*(i)*
It is time they did something about it. For all the hard work you do you deserve more.	*(i)*

Page 93

B2 *c* In evaluating the appropriacy of the respective speeches students should make use of the criteria they devised as a result of the discussion suggested above.

SECTION 3 – *SUMMARY*

In this section students will:

- practise making notes from reading.
- practise presenting a proposal to a group and giving clear and persuasive explanations.
- learn to guess the meaning of unknown words by:
  a using word-formation clues
  b using the context
- learn to identify words important for the understanding of a text.

Teaching tips

Page 94

To describe experiments successfully students need to be familiar with certain core vocabulary.

Supplementary exercise

Ask your students to read through the passage 'Insect Fighters Gear for War' and underline all the verbs associated with conducting experiments.

Among the verbs they may mention are:

developed	predict	tested	is being tested
verified	forecast	agreed with	put
be targeting	was tested	finding from	describe
possibilities	observe	determine	use
			control

A1 Students should be reminded that they can choose any natural pests and not just insects as the title suggests.

Page 96

A3 Before any of the groups begin their presentations students should discuss what they think constitutes a successful proposal. They should then, by referring back to the text, draw up a list of criteria by which they can evaluate the different proposals.

B2 Students need to be aware that sometimes a prefix can be added to a base which may not be a separate word in its own right. 'Indiscriminately' is a good example of this. By removing the prefix *in* we are left with a separate word *discriminately*. *Dis* is often used as a prefix. However, in this case it is not. If we take away *dis* we are left with *criminately* which is not a word in itself.

Supplementary exercise

Construct the following tables of common prefixes and suffixes on the blackboard.

	Prefixes	Example
co (con/ col/c/ cor)	= with/together	
de/dis	= not/opposite of/ away from	
ex	= former/out of	
fore/pre	= before/in front of	
in (im/ il/ir)	= not	
inter	= between/from one to another	
mis/mal	= badly/wrongly	
post	= after	
re	= again/back to	
sub	= under/less than	
super	= over / more than	
sur	= extra	
trans	= across	
un	= not/opposite of/ away from	
able/ ible/ uble	= possible to be	
cide	= killing	

ee	= person receiving an action
ster/ eer/ist	= person doing/ involved in
ful	= with
ize/ ify/en	(also spelt 'ise') = make/become
ish	= resembling
less	= without
let	= small

Ask the students to copy them into their books and then ask them to complete the examples column with as many words containing prefixes and suffixes as they can find from the text 'Harvesting poison'.

Some of the words the students may identify are:

subtropics
reproduced
suicide

Make sure they understand why words like 'informed' and 'predators' do not fall into this category.

When the students have completed as much of the table using examples from the text as they can, ask them to complete the rest of the table using examples of their own. They can then test each other on the meanings of the different examples they have selected.

Students commonly make errors in identifying and using a word in the correct context by failing to determine which part of speech it is. It is a good idea to give them plenty of practice in this skill.

Supplementary exercise

Underline the words given below from the first paragraph of the passage 'Harvesting poison' on page 97.

poisons (*n*)
bitterly (*adv*)
new (*adj*)
combat (*v*)
problems (*n*)
alive (*adv*)

Then ask the students to say which part of speech they represent.

Now ask the students to find at least one example of each part of speech from the third paragraph.

Then ask each student working on their own to underline six words from any part of the text.

Finally, ask them to test each other on their ability to identify the part of speech of the underlined word.

SECTION 4 – *SUMMARY*

In this section students will be engaged in:

- designing promotional literature to explain and persuade.
- preparing a set of arguments in favour of or against a particular plan of action.
- presenting arguments to a group in a formal situation.
- assessing arguments for and against, in order to come to a decision.
- commenting on a decision from a particular point of view.

Teaching tips

Page 97

A Some students may need more help in understanding the information about the potato.
You may like to ask the following questions:
What advantages does the potato have?
What problems do farmers in developing countries face?

Supplementary exercise

Before designing the promotional literature, students might like to try this exercise. Refer to the extract entitled 'The potato' on page 98.

1 The first paragraph demonstrates the writer's intention
A To make the reader aware of a new and exciting range of potato products.
B To show the versatility of the potato.
C To show the high cost of producing convenience foods.
D To show producers the rewards of potato growing.

2 The section about the Irish famine
A cautions against the excessive consumption of potatoes.
B cautions against the excessive production of potatoes.
C supports the case for growing more potatoes.
D suggests that potatoes can cause diseases.

3 The main purpose of the section 'Third World proliferation' is
A to explain the rapid growth of potato production in Asia.
B to show the nutritional benefits of the potato.
C to show the industrial uses of the potato.
D to explain the decrease in potato production in Europe.

4 The diagram illustrating crop production demonstrates that
A potato production exceeds rice production.
B the total production of beans has declined.
C production of potatoes exceeds production of sweet potatoes by over 300%
D the increase in potato production is roughly three times the rate of population growth.

5 From the section 'Top food crop for energy' we can infer that
A one hectare of potatoes produces more edible energy than any other crop.
B potatoes contain more proteins, vitamins and trace elements than rice.
C maize is less nutritious than yams.
D the egg plant is the least useful crop.

Answers: **1** *C* **2** *B* **3** *A* **4** *D* **5** *A*

There is a danger that in completing this task students may become too concerned with content at the expense of presentation.
Ask them to look at the leaflet on the potato.

- Which parts are most relevant in persuading farmers and ministry officials to grow more potatoes?
- Which parts are not appropriate and even irrelevant?

Before dividing students into groups to devise their promotional literature the class should agree on a checklist that determines the effectiveness and persuasiveness of a particular piece of advertising literature.

On completing their leaflets they should then circulate them around the class and evaluate them according to the criteria that the class agreed upon.

Page 100

B One possible difficulty with this activity is that students may feel that they have insufficient background information to complete it. In similar sections of some previous units they have had a considerably greater amount of background information.

In introducing the activity you should point out that you are not concerned with the techniques of rice milling but the impact of change and progress on various groups of people.

The introductory activities of **B1**, **B2**, **B3** should help the students prepare for the major task by contextualising this universal human dilemma in a familiar setting. The students should then be able to see the problem through the eyes of the various interest groups they have opted to represent.

Page 100

C1 Some students may not immediately recognise the problems identified in the introductory scenario and it may be necessary to elicit them by asking questions.
Until recently who did most of the rice milling in Bangladesh?
How did they do it?
Who does it now?
What have been the positive effects of this?
Why is it a problem?
Some of the points students may mention during the discussion are:

- visual appeal.
- concise use of language.
- use of diagrams.
- clear and effective use of headings and sub-headings.

Page 101

C2 In preparing the three different accounts each group may tend to concentrate just on giving their view of the outcome.

It is important that they remember that the style of writing will vary for the three different tasks.

Supplementary exercise

Ask the students to identify which of the three accounts these extracts are probably taken from.

- After thoroughly examining the facts presented to them, the Ministry officials wisely opted to embark on a new era of prosperity and progress.
- The greater cost-effectiveness achieved by using the new methods of production on balance outweighed the short term effects on certain sections of the rural workforce.
- The little man doesn't have a chance when they can spend all that money on advertising.

Answers: *b*, *c*, *a*.

SECTION 5

It is vital that students learn to transfer the techniques of effectively presenting information into their own subject specialisms. Try to ensure that they become proficient in organising study groups. Then they should be able to do this themselves before any important public examinations when it is vital that they revise efficiently.

TEST PRACTICE

Interview skills

In many units of this book the students are asked to talk about various aspects of their countries, hometowns or areas. People are often unaware of what is interesting about their homeland. The exercises that follow aim to sensitize students more to their surroundings, to excite their imaginations and enable them to paint an accurate picture for the outsider.

In many interview situations candidates are often asked about their home environment in order to test their descriptive and communicative skills.

A Ask students if any of the following features of their home environment would be of particular interest to an outsider.

1	landscape	*9*	crops
2	architecture	*10*	vegetation
3	dress	*11*	pace of life
4	customs	*12*	handicrafts
5	people	*13*	colours
6	language	*14*	wildlife
7	climate	*15*	smells
8	food	*16*	entertainment

B Ask students to match the following list of details with the list of features in **A**.

a rolling hills
b brightly coloured robes
c street games, *e.g.* bowls, chess . . .
d acres of green tobacco
e sweltering hot nights
f delicately woven baskets
g deep greens and blues
h vast sandy expanses
i towering office blocks
j stalls laden with multi-coloured fruit
k torrents of rain
l rows of small red-brick houses
m a white blanket of snow
n the sweet scent of apple blossom

C Now give the students the following list of adjectives and ask them which of the features in **A** they would associate them with. Note that it is quite likely that many students will make very different associations since the images they have in their minds are certain to vary.

crisp	melting	daunting
pungent	light-hearted	airy
tight	pastel	striking
wide open	abundant	intricate
extravagant	exotic	smoky
imposing	breathtaking	sad
sharp	soft	radiant
enclosed	fine	jabbering
delicate	jovial	elegant

Encourage students to check the meanings of any of these terms in a dictionary if they are new to them.

Ask students to add to this list any descriptive words or phrases that would be useful for describing their own home environment.

D Ask students to choose five of the features listed in **A** which they feel are the most interesting aspects of their homes.

Students should now be encouraged to write one or two sentences per feature to paint a vivid picture of their homes.

Ask students to read each other's sentences and comment on whether the places sound interesting, or not.

E The following list of questions could now be used to test students' ability to answer questions of this kind in an interview situation.

The teacher may pose these questions randomly to the class in rapid succession.

On the other hand, the teacher may prefer to use them in one-to-one interview practice.

- Where do you come from?
- Would you advise a tourist to go there?
- What would you pick out from your home area as being of particular interest?
- What is the landscape like?
- Is there anything special about the architecture?
- What kind of crops are grown there?
- How would you describe the climate?
- Would you say that there was anything special about the people?
- What type of souvenirs would a tourist buy?
- Would you recommend any particular food?
- How do people spend their free time?
- What are the chief festivals?
- What language is most commonly spoken?

UNIT 6 · *Brave new world*

INTRODUCTION — WHY BIOTECHNOLOGY?

Students, and indeed teachers, may well ask how the topic of Biotechnology is relevant to their work.

It should be stressed that in this, as in other units, the topic is secondary to the overall teaching objectives. This is to say that teachers and students should be aware that the main objective is not to teach about Biotechnology, but to teach certain skills through materials on this topic.

At the same time, most people would agree that Biotechnology is both interesting and topical for students, whatever their discipline. It has world-wide implications for citizens of all societies.

The rights and wrongs of Biotechnology and Genetic Engineering are very much in question today. This unit will provide your students with the opportunity to become acquainted with the issues involved.

OBJECTIVES OF THIS UNIT

Here we are mainly concerned with two things:

1 Teaching students to recognise bias in reading and listening material. Students are thus encouraged to be aware of the force of language, the purpose of text, and who it is intended for in a wide variety of texts.

2 Encouraging students to adopt more colourful language so that their own powers of expression in writing and speaking are more effective.

Throughout the Unit a number of other study and exam skills are taught and practised. These are listed below, section by section.

SECTION 1 — *SUMMARY*

In this section students will:

- learn to recognise emotive language.
- learn to assess whether emotive language is extreme or moderate, pessimistic or optimistic.
- learn to employ negative emotive language in writing a short paragraph.
- practise describing a graph, summarising trends and explaining predictions.

The pictures and texts at the beginning of the unit introduce students to the idea that societies and civilisations are constantly changing, rising and falling. Later on in the unit students consider the future of present civilisations.

Teaching tips

Page 103
Start off by asking students:

– What are these pictures of?
– Where would you find these objects?
– Can you name the civilisation they come from?

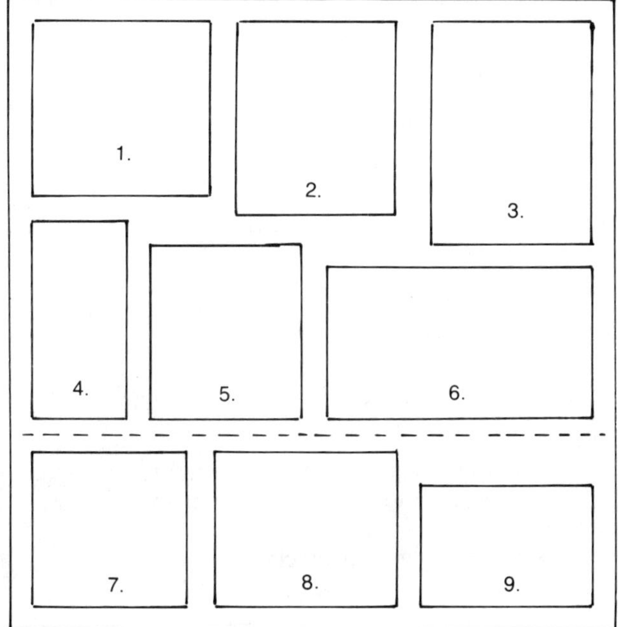

1 Sumerian
2 Egyptian
3 Arab (Moorish)
4 Greek
5 Confucian
6 Norman
7 Sumerian
8 Thai Buddhist
9 Aztec

Before students read the passage, ask them to read the titles and subtitles on this page. Then ask:

– What do you expect this passage and the unit to be about?
– What does 'on the way down' mean in this context?

Encourage students to quickly skim the passage on page 103 and the unit as a whole to answer these questions.

Now get students to work through questions **A1–4**. Keep the discussion in **A4** short.

Supplementary exercise

If you feel that students are having difficulty in dealing with the lexis of the text on page 103, try this exercise.

1 In the passage on page 103 find words which mean:
– fell
– highly developed
– degeneration

Answers: collapsed/sophisticated/run down

2 Find examples in the text of:
– artefacts
– disasters

Answers:
artefacts - pyramids, the sphinx, an arch, stone constructions
disasters - earthquakes, fires

3 Are artefacts
a objects of natural beauty?
b things made by humans?

Answer: *b*

4 Think of other examples of artefacts and disasters and extend your lists.

Page 104

B1/2 should be done quickly. To speed work up, each extract could be examined by a different group.

Supplementary exercise

Page 105

B4 focuses on the vocabulary of the three texts on pages 104–5. If you find students are slow to suggest more neutral phrases, ask them to do this exercise.
The answers are given in brackets.

Find a more extreme version of these phrases in the extracts on pages 104–5.

1. have led to problems in our society
   (have brought the human species to the verge of self-destruction)
2. racial problems
   (race-hatred)
3. nuclear disaster
   (nuclear Armageddon)
4. the division between the rich and the poor grows
   (the gulf widens between those who have too much and those who have too little)
5. more difficult times are coming
   (We are heading for a period of human misery on a scale quite unprecedented)
6. the rich took wealth from others
   (the rich were those who plundered by conquest)
7. we were becoming rich at the expense of our children
   (we were stealing from posterity)
8. Now we have to start paying the costs.
   (The accounting is about to begin.) The point is emphasised by ending with the word 'begin', making the sentence more dramatic.

Page 105

B5 Students may need some oral preparation for the writing task in **B5***a*.
Ask students to study the picture in groups and agree on the three most extreme or most worrying images.

(*e.g.* over-population, pollution, alcoholism, etc.)

Take an aspect that most groups have picked out and ask all groups in the class to think of some phrases or sentences to describe it.

Put the resulting phrases on the blackboard and ask students to decide which are the most extreme.

Ask students to plan and write their paragraph in groups.

Page 105

C1 This graph is based on actual research. However, the trends shown here are extreme and may surprise many students. It should perhaps be noted that students do not have to agree with them. They are only required to describe them for now.

The teacher could refer students back to work done on trends in Unit 4, since some of that language is recycled here.

When students have completed **C1***b* tell them to compare their conclusions in small groups. This should provide some useful recycling of graph language.

A brief presentation could be made to the class by a spokesperson from one of the groups.

Supplementary exercise

If it becomes clear that some students are having difficulty with the language, the following gapped exercise could be presented, attempted and discussed.

The level of difficulty of this exercise can be adjusted by:

- giving the alternatives as they are above (without the italics).
- jumbling the order of the pairs.
- jumbling all the alternatives.

Read through the text which follows and choose a phrase from the box below to fill each gap.

This graph paints a very ...**1**... picture of our future world. The population, pollution, food per capita and industrial output curves show ...**2**... trends. Up to now they have been ...**3**..., and they will continue to do so until the early part of the 21st century, when they will ...**4**.... After this, according to the graph, they will all ...**5**....

The curves for death and birth rates have a similar shape. They have both ...**6**... to date and will continue to do so until the start of the 21st century, when they ...**7**... reach a trough. After that, they will both increase ...**8**....

The resources curve shows an overall ...**9**... from the beginning of the 20th century to the end of the 21st. This fall is a gradual one until the ...**10**... of the 20th century. A drastic decline will follow and continue ...**11**... the mid 21st century. Then there will be a ...**12**....

1	*bleak*/rosy	**7**	*will*/have
2	different/*similar*	**8**	*rapidly*/slowly
3	falling gradually/*rising steadily*	**9**	increase/*decline*
4	*reach a peak*/bottom out	**10**	*end*/beginning
5	rise dramatically/*decline sharply*	**11**	*until*/after
6	climbed steeply/*fallen steadily*	**12**	renewed increase/ *levelling off*

SECTION 2 — *SUMMARY*

In this section we continue to look at the predicament of modern society, focusing here on the positive effects of one technological innovation, Biotechnology.

Students will:

- learn to pick out optimistic language in reading and listening.
- practise skimming texts for main points, for text organisation, for information and for bias.
- practise making notes on texts in mind map form.
- practise identifying target readers/listeners and the purpose of the text.
- learn to differentiate between fact and opinion.
- practise employing positive emotive language in writing a short passage.

Teaching tips

Page 107

As an introduction of this section, draw students attention to the title and the writing on the blackboard on page 107. Then ask students what they expect Section 2 to be about.

Page 107

B1 Some of the questions in exercise **B1** will probably be difficult for students. The teacher should emphasise that it does not matter if students do not know the answers. They are contained within the text. Therefore push the students through these questions quickly.

Remind students to make notes on the questions they can answer, or are willing to guess at.

Page 109

B3 In exercise **B3***b* students are asked to skim the text to locate the sentences containing the main points.

After the students have made an attempt at this, the teacher might mention the following rule of thumb:

- Very often the main point of a paragraph is summed up in the first sentence. So, if students want to get a quick impression of what a text is about, they should read the first sentence of each paragraph.
- However, this does not always work and sometimes students have to scrutinise a paragraph more closely to find the main point.

This text illustrates both the rule and the exception in that the main points of the first three paragraphs are quite difficult to find. But the main points of the remaining paragraphs are all contained in the first sentences.

Remind students that the technique of skimming for main points is a very important one. As exercise **B3***c* will show, it makes note-making easier, since by finding the main points students will find it easier to decide on main headings/key words.

Locating the main points of a text is also important in English language exams, such as IELTS, where students have to get the gist of a text without reading all of it in detail.

If students are well trained in this technique it can save them valuable time, as they will not always feel the need to read every text thoroughly.

In exercise **B3***c* it is important that students note the instruction to leave enough space on their mind maps to add further details later.

If students need reminding of mind map techniques, refer them back to Unit 4.

In exercise **B3***e*, check that students:

- use arrows correctly.
- distinguish between main headings, sub-headings and detail.
- group related ideas together.

Make it clear that mind maps are a personal form of notemaking and will therefore differ from student to student.

Supplementary exercise

It is worth pointing out to students that the text on pages 108–109 is difficult for two reasons.

Firstly, it contains a lot of technical vocabulary and, if we are not familiar with the topic, we will find this text difficult. Words like 'biotechnology', 'genetic engineering', 'recombinant DNA', 'biological prosthetics' and 'messenger RNA' are really only comprehensible to people working in that field. This is a problem for native speakers as well as foreign language learners and we must all learn not to baulk at such technical vocabulary. Students should realise that we do not have to understand all the words in a text in order to grasp the general meaning.

The second reason why this text might be difficult is that students with a less developed general vocabulary may encounter problems because there are a number of difficult general words. This exercise focuses on these.

It is possible that the twelve words and phrases listed below may hinder a student's comprehension of the first three paragraphs of the text. Below are also listed a group of words and phrases, some of which are good substitutes for the phrases from the text in this context.

From the focus words and phrases choose the ones that you wish to concentrate on and write them on the blackboard.

Opposite them, write up the possible substitutes.

Ask students to find and examine the words in the text and decide what part of speech they are (*e.g.* noun/verb/adjective).

Next, ask students to choose a suitable substitute. Note that here, for the teacher's convenience, we have put the correct substitute (in italics) and distractor immediately after each focus word. When you put these on the blackboard, you should omit this distinction and jumble them.

This exercise can be continued by asking each group of students to take one or two of the subsequent paragraphs of the text and to select a small number of focus words, which they think are difficult.
With the help of a dictionary, they should find a suitable substitute and an incorrect one for each word.
Students' exercises could then be presented to the rest of the class as further practice.

Focus words	Line	Suggested substitutes
encompasses	1	*includes*/surrounds
diverse	1	*varied*/similar

Focus words	**Line**	**Suggested substitutes**
yields	3	*production*/produces
process	3	deal with/*operation*
stem from	4	stalk/*come from*
disparate	5	*different*/same
blossoming	8	*expansion*/flowering
interconnected	9	relation/*related*
synthesized	15	*formed*/destroyed
partially	17	*to some extent*/completely
introduced	19	*put*/made known
sealing off	21	stop/*closing off*

Pages 111 and 112

D1 Note that this exercise requires students to skim all three texts on pages 111 to 113.

D2/3/4 These questions refer only to the texts they accompany.

Page 113

D4 If students have not come across the idea of 'discussing levels of certainty' before, they may find this a difficult exercise.

Before doing **D4** the teacher could introduce the idea with the following exercise.

Supplementary exercise

Ask students: How certain is it that it will rain tomorrow? Is it very certain, probable or just possible?

1 I'm sure it will rain tomorrow.
2 It might rain tomorrow, so we'd better take coats.
3 It hasn't rained for days, so it should rain tomorrow.
4 He thought it would rain tomorrow.
5 It could rain tomorrow but I hope it doesn't.
6 It may rain tomorrow, though I doubt it.
7 There is no question but that it will rain tomorrow.

Suggested answers:
certain — 1, 7
probable — 3, 4
possible — 2, 5, 6

Supplementary exercise

The three texts on pages 111–113 are rich in descriptive language.
The following is a supplementary exercise which focuses on the collocation of certain adjectives and nouns in text 1. It asks students to decide which adjectives and nouns can be used together.

Present the two axes, **Nouns** and **Descriptive phrases** as below, to the students.

Ask the students to examine text 1, page 111, and to tick the combinations of nouns and descriptive phrases that they find there.

Next ask the students to tick, in a different colour, any other combinations they feel are possible.
Students should leave blank any combinations they feel are impossible. This should provide the basis for interesting discussion and investigation.

Finally present the answers given below to the students as a check. Note that some of these answers are open to discussion.

Students could now be encouraged to do similar exercises with texts 2 and 3 on pages 113 and 114.

Nouns

Descriptive phrases	stream	steel	world	technologies	balance	mystery	importance	way	quantities	substances	range	amounts	knowledge	chemicals	body	disease	organisms	race
endless	√		•			•			•		•	•	•					
gleaming		√	•						•	•					•			
topsy-turvy			√					√										
smelly	•		•						•	•				•	•		•	
sad			•			•		•								•		•
new		•	•	√		•	•	•	•	•	•	•	•	•	•	•	•	•
delicate					√			•		•				•	•		•	•
sinister			•	•		√	•	•		•				•		•	•	
real			•			•	√	•		•				•				
natural	•		•		•	•	•	√	•	√				•	•	•	•	•
rare				•					•	√		•	•	•		•	•	•
large	•						•	•	√		•	•			•		•	•
whole	•		•								√				•		•	•
minute	•							•	•		•	√			•		•	•
detailed								•			•		√					
toxic	•								•	•				√				
human													•		√	√	√	√
living										•					•		√	

Key √ = combination found in text
• = other possible combinations

Page 115

D7 This is intended as a fun exercise. Therefore encourage students to be outrage-

ous and to have a go at using some of the very positive language they have encountered in this section.
Text 3 on page 113 can be used as a model.

Encourage students also to refer to the collocation tables they have drawn up.

SECTION 3 – *SUMMARY*

In this section students will:

- learn to identify the attitude of speakers, both through the language that they use and their tone.
- learn to anticipate what someone is going to say from what they already know about the attitude of the speaker.
- practise identifying the bias of a wide variety of texts.
- learn to agree and disagree in appropriate ways.
- practise putting their views in a meeting.
- practise expressing their opinion in concise written form.

Teaching tips

Page 115

A This exercise provides an opportunity for students to voice their personal opinion in reaction to the issues raised so far. This can either be done in a full class discussion or in groups. It is intended as a brief warm-up exercise.

B In this exercise play **parts 1 and 2** of the tape only.

Page 117

C2 The aim of this exercise is to get students to anticipate what they are likely to hear on the tape. Note that they are going to hear the second part of the interview first heard in **B**.

In exercise **C2***a* give students a few minutes to think about what the speaker might say about patenting. Ask them to guess some specific points that the speaker might make.

List the points that the students come up with on the blackboard. These can act as a checklist for exercise **C2***b*.

After listening, examine the list on the blackboard with the students and agree which points were actually raised.

Page 117

D The 'Complete Picture' contains a number of texts from a variety of sources. The exercises on these texts are designed to simulate a real study situation, where students are drawing on and assessing the usefulness of a number of texts.

Before starting exercise **D2** ask students to read through the instructions for the task in their books.

Ask them to decide how many texts each group/student will look at.

Next ask students to consider the fact that questions **D2***a*, *b* and *c* refer to all texts. They will have to decide:

– whether they will constantly refer back to these questions on page 117 for each text.
– whether these questions should be put on the blackboard for ease of reference.
– whether each student will make a note of the questions and refer to this while reading.

Since this is an exercise in rapid reading, skimming and scanning, it is important that students should be under a time pressure.
Therefore set a suitable time limit for your students to complete **D2**.

Page 127

E1 This exercise refers back to the listening at the beginning of this section.
Exercise **E1***a* leads students to the idea that by agreeing first with a speaker, and then disagreeing, the disagreement is more polite.
Exercise **E1***b* leads students to conclude that by disagreeing immediately, the response sounds less polite.

Page 128

E5 The writing task at the end of this section is important. Firstly, it is an opportunity for students to consolidate their ideas on the whole issue discussed to date.
Secondly, in terms of writing skills, it is an opportunity for the teacher to offer guidance in planning an 'opinion' type essay. This technique is required by many English language exams.
If you feel that your students need help in writing opinion essays, you might like to try the following approach.

Supplementary exercise

Put the students in groups according to
– which topic they discussed in **E3/4**.
– the position they took (*i.e.* for, against or 'on the fence').
Ask each group to suggest a basic plan for an essay on their topic.
Discuss the plans with the class, pointing out strengths and weaknesses.
Suggest this model plan for any opinion essay:

1 State your opinion on the issue, either for, against, undecided or examining both sides.
2 Give at least two examples to back up your opinion with supporting details for each.
3 Briefly outline arguments which could be used by those holding a different opinion and rebut these arguments.
4 Restate your original opinion in different, and if possible, stronger terms.

Ask students to replan their essays using these guidelines.
An example plan might look like this:

Topic Scientists should have free rein in their research.
Plan
1 ... strongly oppose the idea that ...
2 *e.g. 1* Scientists can be irresponsible.
   – more interested in fame, money, etc. than safety.
   – do dangerous experiments *e.g.* genetic engineering.
   e.g. 2 Scientists are uncontrolled.
   – politicians have no power over scientists.
   – public does not understand science.
   – too much money spent on science (space, superconductors) and not enough on basic human needs.
3 It may be said that
   – scientists best qualified to determine area of research but
   – does not mean should be allowed complete freedom.
4 Governments must exercise more control over scientists.

SECTION 4 – *SUMMARY*

In this section students will be encouraged to employ the skills and language learned and practised throughout this unit in a natural, life-like way. Students will be engaged in:

– discussion and debate.
– writing to present a point of view.
– responding to biased writing.
– making oral presentation.

This is a fluency activity and it is important that students are carried along by enthusiasm and interest. The teacher should therefore ensure that students are not too concerned about accuracy.

Impose time limits on the activities to encourage this attitude.

Teaching tips

Page 130

If you do decide to record **Step 4** Air play, you will probably find that students will be very interested in hearing their programmes again, and those of other groups. This can be very motivating and provide a nice opportunity for listening for pleasure.

You might introduce an element of competition by asking an outsider to listen to the recordings and judge the effectiveness of the programmes.

SECTION 5

Teaching tips

Page 131

A Identifying bias

How the teacher organises this work will depend on the nature of the class.

If, for example, all students are taking the same subjects, then one area could be agreed upon and worked on by the class as a whole.

If, on the other hand, the class is not a homogenous one, students will have to be divided up according to their subjects. They may be able to work in small groups or they may have to work on their own.

B Your own position

For motivational reasons, it is important that somebody reads the students' summaries. Although it would be interesting if this could be done within the English class, it may prove difficult. In this case, the students should be encouraged to ask a subject colleague outside the English group to comment.

C/D are really concerned with making students sensitive to language that they hear around them.

If the teacher feels that the students need further practice in observing other people's choice of language, tone of voice and facial expression and gestures, a video tape might profitably be used here. This could be of anything, a televised university lecture, a political speech, a discussion programme, a comedy or a drama programme.

Students might try to record, on video or tape, lectures, talks and discussions in their own subjects, which could provide further material for analysis.

This should be relatively easy to organise and very motivating because it takes the English class into the subject classroom, and brings subject material back to the English classroom.

TEST PRACTICE

READING

Section 1

Choose a sentence *A*, *B*, *C* or *D* which is closest in meaning to the original sentence.

(*NB* All these sentences appear in Unit 6. The exact references are given for each.)

1 (Page 108, para 1, lines 7–10)
The blossoming of applied biology is due to important advances in many fields.
A Because applied biology has grown so rapidly, advances are being made in many other fields.
B Progress in the applied sciences has reached a plateau and does not promise great advances for some time to come.
C In spite of the main attention being given to the development of other fields of science, applied biology has managed to flourish.
D As a result of progress in many linked areas, applied biology has developed and will continue to do so.

2 (Page 108, para 5, lines 2–4)
... means that they (the new products) can be obtained in essentially pure form and hence are free from other toxic products.
A The new products are completely natural.
B The new products are used to eradicate toxic.
C The new products contain few impurities.
D The new products are potentially poisonous.

3 (Page 108, para 6, lines 4–5)
Should this prove possible, the savings in terms of fertiliser and improved soil fertility will be enormous.
A It is certain that costs will be reduced in agriculture.
B It is hoped that great savings can be made in agriculture.
C It is expected that spending on agriculture will be reduced.
D It is doubtful that agricultural costs will fall in the future.

4 (Page 109, para 1, lines 5–6)
It is conceivable that similar techniques may be used.
A Similar techniques are to be used.
B Under no circumstances could similar techniques be used.
C People fear that similar techniques may be used.
D Similar techniques might possibly be used.

5 (Page 109, para 3, lines 2–3)
Scientists themselves are currently reluctant to commit themselves to specific predictions.
A Scientists are not sure about the exact timing of future developments.
B Scientists are at present engaged in experiments that they feel sure will yield immediate results.
C Scientists are sure that this work will bring advances.
D Scientists hesitate to commit themselves to work of this kind.

6 (Page 109, para 4, lines 2–3)
It offers immediate and attractive prospects for developing countries.
A It appeals to developing countries only.
B It can benefit developing countries from the start.
C The prospective market in developing countries is huge.
D Developing countries are especially suited to it.

Section 2

Read this passage and choose one word that best fills the gap on each line. If no word is required, choose the option that is indicated by a blank (. . .)
NB This is the text that appears on page 119 of Unit 6.

		A	*B*	*C*	*D*
7	A patent must first of .... be new. No other inventor must	foremost	everything	things	all
8	have .... a patent on the same invention, and nobody must have published the discovery before filing for a patent, although in the US there is a "grace period" of	made	filed	taken	done

		A	*B*	*C*	*D*
9	.... to a year between publishing and filing a patent. The next criterion	up	over	less	...
10	.... patenting is that an invention	with	of	for	to
11	.... involve a truly inventive step. Routine, trivial or unexpected modifications of an existing technology therefore	shouldn't	can	can't	must
12	do not .... as fulfilling what the patent attorneys call the "inventive step". This is often the	help	count	consist	seem
13	.... that lawyers end up arguing about in the courts. The court then has to decide	criterion	argument	news	fact
14	.... the invention is obvious "to someone skilled in the art". Biotechnology is	that	...	whether	about
15	.... a new industry that patent lawyers often try to convince a court that something is inventive	not	such	still	...
16	.... because the technology is so new and "unobvious". The recent court	since	as	through	merely
17	.... in Britain between Genentech and Wellcome indicated that the court was not prepared to treat biotechnology	...	order	case	trial

		A	B	C	D
18	any .... than other technologies. For a patent office to grant a patent, the invention must be industrially	other	more	differently	different
19	....	applicable	available	produced	...

Section 3

These questions all refer to the texts on pages 111–114 of Unit 6.

Text 1 (Page 111)

20 What is the general view of market analysts concerning the biotechnology industry?
A an optimistic one
B a pessimistic one
C one of hopelessness
D no view

21 The author's reference to the 'topsy turvy world'
A means that the world is being upset by biotechnology.
B means that our world is already a strange place.
C indicates that our world is in a sad condition.
D suggests that the wonders of biotechnology will correct any inadequacies in our world.

22 What seems to impress the author most about biotechnology?
A Its benefits to the agricultural industry.
B Its solution to the fuel problem.
C Its usefulness in the medical world.
D Its lack of reliance on chemicals.

23 The author mentions one reservation about biotechnology. This is that
A it relies heavily on chemicals and drugs.
B it could destroy nature.
C it will not be developed for a long time to come.
D it involves interfering with living organisms.

Text 2 (Page 113)

24 When describing the new advances the author emphasises
A the time that growth takes.
B the size the animals grow.
C neither size nor time.
D both size and time.

25 What stage was the 'transgenic sheep' experiment at when this article was written?
A successful completion
B very early stages
C nearing completion
D not yet started

26 What is the attitude of Trevor Scott to the new 'transgenic sheep'?
A pessimistic about its success
B unsure of the value of such an experiment
C confident of 100% success
D wholly in favour of the experiment

Text 3 (Page 113)

27 How does the writer feel about the standards of genetically engineered products?
A confident of a high standard
B doubtful about safety standards
C desires stricter tests
D insists that higher standards can and must be achieved

28 What did the results of the clinical trials show?
A The new drug is 100% safe.
B Reactions to the new drug were less than those caused by other drugs.
C Reactions to the new drug were similar to those caused by other drugs.
D There were considerable reactions to the new drug.

29 What seems to interest the writer of this article most?
A Ridding the world of Hepatitis B.
B Improving the standards of medicine.
C Finding alternative methods for combatting Hepatitis B.
D Promoting one particular product.

Questions on all three texts

For the following questions you need to look again at the three texts on pages 111–114 of Unit 6.

30 In contrast to texts 1 and 2, text 3
A is not concerned with future developments of biotechnology.
B is only concerned with future developments of biotechnology.
C is concerned with dangers posed by biotechnological developments.
D is concerned with a variety of areas which can benefit from biotechnology.

31 In contrast to the writers of texts 2 and 3, the writer of text 1 is mainly interested in
A one single application of genetic engineering.
B two applications of genetic engineering.
C three applications of genetic engineering.
D several applications of genetic engineering.

32 The three texts agree on the following point:
A Genetic engineering has a lot to offer the medical profession.
B Genetic engineering should be treated with caution.
C Genetic engineering is something that can benefit man.
D Genetic engineering can revolutionise the agricultural industry.

LISTENING

Section 1 — Choosing from diagrams

In this exercise you will need to look at diagrams and pictures in Unit 6 and the multiple choice answers here.

In each case listen carefully, to the question your teacher reads you, find the relevant picture, then choose the answer you think is best.

1 *A* Picture 1
B Picture 2
C Picture 5
D Picture 8

2 *A* Picture 3
B Picture 6
C Picture 7
D Picture 9

3 *A* food per capita
B population
C birth rate
D resources

4 *A* Bacteria for use in waste treatment and pollution control
B Gene therapy for diseases such as sickle cell anaemia
C Understanding of immunological processes
D Petrochemical substitutes

5 *A* Wellcome
B Medical Research Council
C Genetech
D British Biotechnology Limited

6 *A* 01–6365222
B 01–6365422
C 01–3635422
D 01–6365422

7

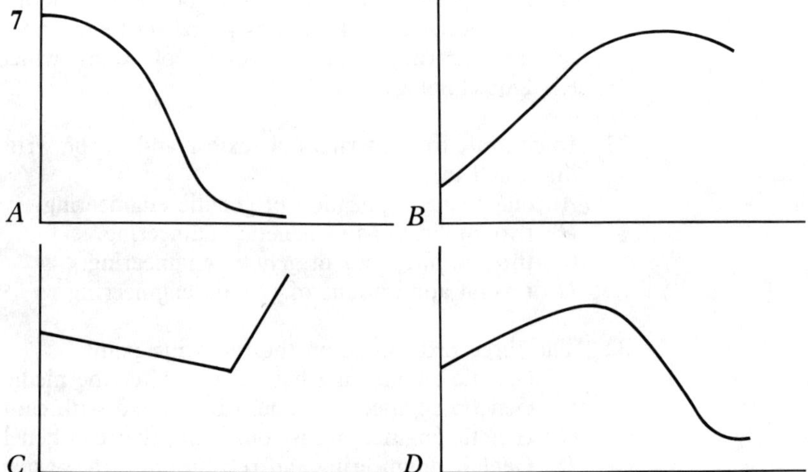

Section 2 — Listening to different opinions

For this section, and for section 4, you need to go back to the listenings in Unit 6. This section consists of questions on the extracts that are first considered on page 111 of Unit 6. Before you start you will need to find the correct place on the tape.

Extract 1

8 The advantage of biological catalysts is
A they work only at high pressures and high temperatures.
B they work only at low pressures and low temperatures.
C they can work at normal pressures and temperatures.

9 Modern washing powders contain
A chemical catalysts.
B biological catalysts.
C no catalysts.

10 Effluents are
A catalysts.
B drinking water.
C liquid waste.

Extract 2

11 If a plant has virus resistance
A it can be damaged by viruses.
B it will get no virus lesions.
C it will be covered by virus lesions.

12 Lesions are
A wounds
B flowers.
C leaves.

13 The interviewee thinks that virus resistance
A definitely will not change the face of agriculture.
B definitely will change the face of agriculture.
C might change the face of agriculture.

Extract 3

14 Biodegradable herbicides are
A good for the soil.
B detrimental to the soil.
C broken down by the soil.

15 Herbicides are
A fertilisers.
B weed-killers.
C crop plants.

Extract 4

16 Does the interviewee believe that you can make leaner beef?
A He feels that it could be possible.
B He feels that we definitely can.
C He feels that it is quite impossible.

Extract 5

17 Hepatitis B
A always causes immediate death.
B inevitably causes cancer of the liver in later years.
C can have serious consequences.

Section 3 — Replying to questions

Choose the best reply to the questions or statements your teacher reads you.

18 *A* I went down town.
B I don't know.
C Yes, I have.
D I live in Darwin.

19 *A* How many do you need?
B I couldn't.
C Sorry, I can't right now.
D I've got no idea.

20 *A* Just down the road.
B It's by the photocopiers.
C It's behind the science building.
D Why don't you try the index?

21 *A* Neither do I.
B They're unbearable.
C I feel great.
D I haven't got a clue.

22 *A* Must you?
B Won't you?
C I couldn't agree more.
D Will I?

23 *A* Let's go at eightish.
B Better late than never.
C Now and again.
D I really don't mind.

Section 4 — Listening to an Interview

This section consists of questions on the interview that was first considered on page 115 of Unit 6. Find the correct place on the tape before you begin. Part 2 – Plain Speaking.

At the end of the first part of the interview answer questions 24–27.

24 The interviewer claims that transferring characteristics from one species to another
A is a completely new concept.
B is the speciality of the interviewee.
C has occurred only in the last 30 years.
D has always happened.

25 The interviewee feels that Genetic Engineering

A reduced the variety of species we have.
B increases the variety of species we have.
C doesn't affect the variety of species we have.
D destroys the variety of species we have.

26 The interviewee's main concern about Genetic Engineering is that it
A is dangerous to human lives.
B is contrary to the laws of nature.
C is cruel to mice.
D encourages smoking.

27 Which of the following adjectives best describes the interviewee's manner of speaking?
A Animated.
B Earnest.
C Ambiguous.
D Collected.

After hearing the second part of the interview (Part 3 on the tape) answer questions 28–31.

28 The attitude of the interviewer towards the interviewee can be described as
A antagonistic and unfriendly.
B disinterested and bored.
C opposed but polite.
D in enthusiastic agreement.

29 Which of the following statements represents the speaker's opinion on the proposals for patenting?
A It was high time that patent office made a decision.
B The patent office's decision was unacceptable.
C It is the patent office's responsibility to protect animals.
D Animals are indistinguishable from manufactured goods in this case.

30 The interviewer feels that
A the interviewee is being absurd.
B the interviewee is being practical.
C the interviewee is being unrealistic.
D the interviewee is being philosophical.

31 Who does the speaker think will benefit most from the patent office's decision?
A Genetic engineers.
B Animals.
C The patent office.
D Farmers.

READING

Section 1	Section 2		Section 3	
1 *D*	7 *D*	13 *A*	20 *A*	26 *D*
2 *C*	8 *B*	14 *C*	21 *A*	27 *A*
3 *B*	9 *A*	15 *B*	22 *C*	28 *C*
4 *D*	10 *C*	16 *D*	23 *D*	29 *D*
5 *A*	11 *D*	17 *C*	24 *D*	30 *A*
6 *B*	12 *B*	18 *C*	25 *C*	31 *B*
		19 *A*		32 *C*

LISTENING

Section 1 – Choosing from diagrams (page 116 in this book)

TO THE TEACHER: Read these sentences aloud **once**. They should be spoken at conversational speed, not dictation speed. Pause for about five seconds after each question.

		Answers
1	Look at the pictures on page 103 in Unit 6. Which picture shows a carving of a head with a bearded face and tied back hair from a side angle?	*A*
2	Which picture shows the ruins of an arched doorway made of stone?	*B*
3	Look at the graph on page 106. Which curve shows a general downward trend?	*D*
4	Look at the table at the bottom of page 109, entitled 'Delphi predictions of biological breakthroughs'. Which of the four breakthroughs listed on the question paper seems to be the most promising, A, B, C or D?	*A*
5	Look at the articles on pages 118–125. Which of the institutions listed on your question paper is not advertised here?	*C*
6	Look at the advert on page 121. Which of the telephone numbers listed on your question paper is to be found in the bottom left-hand corner of the page?	*B*
7	Look at the four graphs on the question paper. Which graph shows a gradual decline followed by a sudden and steady increase?	*C*

Section 2 — Listening to different opinions

Answers

Extract 1	Extract 2	Extract 3
8 *C*	11 *B*	14 *C*
9 *B*	12 *A*	15 *C*
10 *C*	13 *B*	

Extract 4	Extract 5
16 *B*	17 *C*

Section 3 — Replying to questions

TO THE TEACHER: Read these sentences aloud **once** at conversational speed. Pause for five seconds after each question.

		Answers
18	Where have you been?	*A*
19	Could you give me a hand?	*C*
20	Could you tell me where the catalogue is, please?	*B*
21	I can't stand those people. How do you feel about them?	*B*
22	I think I'll stop now.	*A*
23	Shall we eat now or later?	*D*

Section 4 — Listening to an interview

Answers

24	*D*	**28**	*C*
25	*A*	**29**	*B*
26	*B*	**30**	*C*
27	*A*	**31**	*A*

UNIT 7 · *Your good health!*

INTRODUCTION

Whether we are assessing the state of a nation's health, reporting on the effectiveness of a programme, studying educational or governmental policies or considering our own academic progress, the notion of evaluation is a fundamental one.

This Unit takes the idea of evaluation as its main focus and offers students guidance on the steps needed to evaluate objectively. This is an advanced skill and therefore features in this late Unit.

Since one of the major aims of this book is to help students become more independent in their learning, the idea of evaluation is extended to the students' own progress. Students are encouraged to identify their strengths and weaknesses as part of the self-evaluation approach, and to suggest their own solutions for their weaker areas.

OBJECTIVES OF THIS UNIT

Here we are mainly concerned with two things:

1 Teaching students to evaluate data from all available sources, in order to write an objective report.
2 Encouraging students to assess objectively their progress on this course.

SECTION 1 — *SUMMARY*

In this section students will practise scanning a text for particular information.

Teaching tips

Page 133

A1 In defining a healthy person the students are likely to make extensive use of adjectives. This presents a good opportunity to extend their vocabulary.
Draw a table of two columns (titled 'Healthy' and 'Unhealthy' respectively) on the blackboard and ask your students to provide as many examples as they can of adjectives that describe people's health.

The purpose of these preliminary discussion exercises is to get the students thinking about health. It is not necessary to pay too much attention to the 'correctness' of their answers.

Page 133

B2 This exercise may cause problems for the students. If they are having difficulty, point out that although he mentions three categories, he only discusses two. These are 'social ills' and 'quality of life' factors.

B3 For this exercise the groups should be encouraged to consider examples of different types of society which are likely to produce a wide range of possible problems. You might decide to ensure the question is given this degree of coverage by introducing the activity with a few general questions to the class as a whole, such as:

– How can we classify societies?

Suggested answers
Industrialised/industrialising
rich/poor/intermediate
East/West
North/South
Islamic/Christian
Communist/Non-communist
hot/cold/temperate
land-locked/island

– Do you expect there to be different health problems in these different societies? (Answer likely to be 'Yes' for many reasons)

Then allocate particular countries to the groups or ask them to choose a country to discuss. Try to make sure that in each case a different set of 'circumstances' prevails in the country. For example, if two groups choose African countries, it would be more fruitful for further discussion if one discussed an Islamic, economically intermediate country and the other a predominantly Christian, economically poor country.

SECTION 2 — *SUMMARY*

In this section students will:

- practise scanning a text for particular information.
- practise using information from a collection of reference materials in order to conduct an investigation.
- practise recording information in grid form.
- practise writing a short passage based on grid notes.
- practise identifying errors and making suggestions to rectify them.
- learn to write a report by:
  a taking into account the aim of the report.
  b paying attention to organisation, accuracy, clarity, completeness and layout.
  c distinguishing between appropriate and inappropriate tone.

Teaching tips

Page 134

A1 The 12 yardsticks mentioned here are unrelated to the 12 factors mentioned in **B2** of Section 1 above.

There is no correct set of 12 yardsticks. Students should, however, be encouraged to make a definite choice and it should be explained that there are no right or wrong answers.

Page 135

A3 One way of beginning a discussion on this might be to write up on the blackboard a list of the 12 factors mentioned by WHO. Then ask each group to tick on the board the factors they mentioned. The WHO factors with the least number of ticks should then provide the basis for a discussion. (This discussion could be teacher-led if necessary.)

A4 If sufficient library facilities are not available, try to bring a selection of reference materials to class for this exercise.

Guidelines for research skills; suggested answers:

- Types of books: year-books from involved organisations (U.N., WHO, etc.)
- Use of subject index; use of reference section
- Refer to contents page, index

Page 136

B1 Make sure that the countries the class chooses:

- represent a wide variety.
- are spread throughout the world.
- are at different stages of development.

B2/3 These provide further practice in constructing grids (previously dealt with on page 49, Unit 3 A Question of Power).

B4 Again there is no need to pay too much attention to the 'correctness' of the students' answers.

c This is a good opportunity to revise the language of comparison and contrast introduced in Unit 3 A Question of Power.

Page 136

C1 It might be useful to exploit this exercise to revise the vocabulary, particularly adjectives and adverbs, of *anger* and *surprise*. To do this you could draw up a table on the board with four columns (two for anger, 'adjectives' and 'adverbs', and two for surprise, 'adjectives' and 'adverbs').

The class could then be asked to suggest vocabulary items to fill in the columns. This is a good way of extending vocabulary as the collective knowledge of the whole class is always greater than that of the individual student.

C3 There is no correct answer here. It is the students' opinions which are sought.

Page 137

D You may want to distinguish between a report and written work in general. Ask the students whether they write reports, who they think writes reports and what different types of reports there are.

Students are likely to suggest some of the following:

- scientists' lab. reports
- journalists' newspaper reports
- citizens to police reports
- police reports
- teachers' school reports
- chairman's annual company report

Page 138

F This is a good opportunity to discuss tone and the use of tone with the class.

You should look at **F2**, page 139 of the Student's Book for information about this. In addition, Unit 5 provides plenty of examples of how you vary what you say and write depending on who you are communicating with.

If there are many instances of students not identifying the same sentences in **F1** and **F2**, you could begin a discussion to examine the differences in responses by presenting these in tabular form on the blackboard.

You might then focus on the reasons for one alternative being preferable to another. In this, reference would be made again to the passage at **F2**

Page 139

G2 Before the students try to predict the likely effect of the report on the reader, they should decide which of the adjectives in **F2** are most applicable to the report.

SECTION 3 – *SUMMARY*

In this section students will:

- practise scanning a text for specific information.
- practise writing a report on a project.
- practise establishing criteria for evaluation.
- learn to interpret trends from a table of statistics.

Teaching tips

Page 139

A1 Some of the points students may note:

a To improve nutritional status of children under five.

b Women selected by own communities to train as village health workers.

c In own village, by health care personnel using simple practical methods.

d Measuring amount of malnutrition amongst under 5-year-olds before and after programme.

e The programme had failed to alter significantly the rate of malnutrition in village.

f Reluctance of mothers in village to wean children early. Villagers and health workers had totally different perceptions of what constituted 'health'.

Page 141

B Students can exchange their reports and evaluate them according to the criteria on page 137 of the Student's Book.

Page 143

C2 The students' checklist should look something like this:

	Good	Average	Poor
1 Able to work long hours			
2 Willing to listen to advice			
3 Able to answer questions accurately			
4 Able to relate well to patients			
5 Able to make decisions			
6 Cool and calm under stress			
7 Able to work in team			
8 Able to work alone			

Page 143

D It may be a good idea to ask general introductory questions such as:

- Do you think people should be allowed to smoke if they want to?
- Do you think smoking should be banned in public places?
- What do you think can be done to reduce the consumption of cigarettes?

D1*b* Hungary/Soviet Union/Poland – government anti-smoking policies have had no effect.
Bulgaria/Norway/Sweden – government anti-smoking policies have had some effect.

Page 144

D2 Other possible factors may include :

- price of cigarettes
- availability
- peer group pressure
- health-consciousness of society

D3 Teachers may want to revise the use of the present perfect tense and simple past to describe change before the students write this.

SECTION 4 – *SUMMARY*

In this section students will be:

- scanning a large body of text to find information on particular topic areas.
- conducting a group discussion to reach a decision.
- designing effective promotional literature.

Teaching tips

Page 148

Extract C Students may not immediately recognise the intended irony in the poster. You can elicit this by asking:

- Are brain damage and shortened life-span benefits?
- Why do you think the author of the passage calls them benefits?
- What would be a more obvious alternative to benefits?

Page 148

A2 This activity has great potential but certain sensitive areas must be dealt with first.

Firstly, you may be teaching in an institution in which pupils are banned from smoking. Reassure the pupils who represent the smoker's point of view that this does not mean that they are seen as cigarette smokers themselves.

Secondly, they must be reminded that they are not required to argue that smoking is in itself a good thing. The key point of the discussion is to what extent people should be allowed to smoke if they want to.

Finally, the smokers may feel that all the literature on the subject is against them. This is a good opportunity for students to realise the benefits of reading a text from the opposite perspective to the writer.

Students may be surprised that they are required to defend smoking. However the skill of rebutting an argument is a valuable one and this is the skill being practised here. It is a good idea to remind students that a currently fashionable point of view may at a later date be rejected in the light of new evidence.

Page 149

B3 Students should already have devised a set of criteria for evaluating the persuasiveness of an advertisement in Unit 5.

Refer them back to this and ask them to decide whether any changes in the criteria are necessary to complete this task.

As this is an example of negative persuasion, while the potato poster was an example of positive persuasion, two different approaches are made to achieve what are in effect opposite objectives.

Suggest that the students try to decide whether criteria common to both positive and negative campaigns are implemented differently; for example, with reference to visual appeal.

SECTION 5

In this section, the students are actually guided to seek the teacher's assistance if they feel their ability in certain skills needs help rather than practice.

The aim for the students here is to apply the skills of this Unit to a revision seminar for their subject studies. They should measure how well they are able to apply the skills in Column 1 of the Skills Matrix to their subject.

Suggested criteria which the students may come up with include:

Ability to:	much more help needed	more help needed	OK

Note similarities and differences.

TEST PRACTICE

Section 1 Reading

Village health workers and malnutrition

In a number of villages in the Himalayan foothills in India, after two years of using locally recruited village health workers to encourage earlier weaning, and despite the ready availability of food supplies, malnutrition among children remained at nearly 90%.

In developing countries the provision of adequate basic health care **1** small isolated villages presents a major challenge to health workers and is compounded by the limited financial resources available. Thus, priorities must be in areas of health that yield maximum long-term benefits. One **2** area is malnutrition in the under-five-year-old population, which needs to be solved as a preventive measure at village level rather than a costly curative **3** at a hospital or health centre.

In 1976, **4** assess the need and feasibility for a community health programme in the surrounding villages, a community hospital in the Himalayan foothills of north India instituted a pilot study with the assistance of a voluntary health organisation. Malnutrition was the major health problem of the under-five-year-olds. Poverty, diarrhoeal disease, and other chronic illnesses were not the major factors causing malnutrition but rather the failure to begin weaning until the child was at least 12 months of age. This was based on the belief that consuming solid foods at an earlier age would be detrimental to the child's health. Furthermore, **5** the ready availability of food, the children's diets were insufficient in calories. Following **6** findings of the pilot study, the hospital established a community health programme.

A	B	C	D	
with	to	for	out	**1**
this	like	of	such	**2**
one	thing	that	which	**3**
for	it	to	they	**4**
although	because	however	despite	**5**
a	the	. . .	some	**6**

Training the Village Health Workers

A major objective of the programme was to improve the nutritional status of the under-five-year-old children. It was decided that **7** and other health goals would be best achieved by training village health workers, who **8** be women selected by their own communities. They were trained in their villages for 18 months by health care personnel from the **9** established community health programme, most of **10** had nursing experience. The village health workers were taught in small groups **11** flash cards and practical demonstrations that emphasised nutrition, maternity, and child care. Other aspects of primary health care included the control of infection and diarrhoeal diseases and the treatment of simple illnesses. The preparation of food from **12** available cereals for infant feeding was frequently demonstrated. The village health workers served **13** a part-time basis.

A	B	C	D	
this	these	it	one	**7**
can	are	would	will	**8**
recent	newly	late	new	**9**
whom	them	who	they	**10**
by	utilize	using	learning	**11**
nearly	close	home	locally	**12**
on	in	at	for	**13**

Testing the programme

The programme was tested in two phases. In May 1977, the newly established community health programme, assisted by students from a high school in the district and one of the authors, carried out a survey to determine the prevalence of malnutrition in the under-fives, before the training of the Village Health Workers.

Seven villages were selected at random and the village elders contacted. The children under five years of age and their mothers were asked to gather at a central place. Some children were contacted by **14** to the home or the fields. The name, age, and weight were recorded on a child health record.

In 1979, a second survey was carried out under the direction of another of the authors (R.N.R.) to determine the impact the Village Health Workers had had on malnutrition in the under-five-year-olds.

A	*B*	*C*	*D*	
visiting	call	telephone	visits	**14**

15 Which of the following statements best summarises the opening sentence of paragraph 2 in the preceding passage?

A The need to provide adequate health care is unchallenged.
B Limiting the financial resources available for health care is a challenge.
C Allocating the limited resources available for health care is a challenge.
D There is a need to challenge the resources available for health care.

16 The word 'compounded' (line 3, paragraph 2)

A provides added details of the provision of basic health care.
B introduces an added difficulty to the provision of basic health care.
C qualifies the ideas expressed in the first part of the sentence.
D suggests a means of adding to the limited financial resources available.

17 The author argues that the main priority must be to

A yield maximum benefit to patients with long term illnesses.
B choose areas of health that yield the maximum long term benefit with the limited financial resources available.
C give maximum benefits to the areas that yield the most immediate results.
D give immediate benefits to the areas that will have the most lasting results.

18 In paragraph 3 the writer
A assesses the needs and feasibility of a health care programme.
B refers to a needs and feasibility study for a health care programme.
C assesses a needs and feasibility study for a health care programme.
D describes the details of a needs and feasibility study for a health care programme.

19 What is the main reason given for the high level of malnutrition amongst the under fives?
A insufficient food.
B insufficient fluids.
C mistaken beliefs.
D insufficient income.

20 At what age are the children most susceptible to malnutrition?
A 3 months.
B 12 months.
C 18 months.
D 2 years.

21 The villagers' perceptions of their health needs are
A narrowly preventive.
B wider than those of the experts.
C narrower than those of the experts.
D related to their economic circumstances.

Students will need to refer to **Extract A** page 145 of the Student's Book to answer the following questions.

22 By reading the three reports we can conclude that
A lung cancer causes 129,000 deaths per year.
B more smokers die from coronary heart disease than any other cause.
C smokers are more likely to die from one form of cancer than another.
D coronary heart disease kills more smokers than lung-related diseases.

23 According to the Extract, the amount spent on TV advertising by tobacco manufacturers
A was influenced by the amount spent on the anti-smoking campaign.
B influenced the amount spent on the anti-smoking campaign.
C varied in relation to the anti-smoking campaign's expenditure.
D levelled off after an initial rise.

24 The main objective of Proposition P was to
A prohibit smoking in public.
B punish people for smoking in public.
C encourage the public to stop smoking.
D encourage the public to stop smokers.

25 All policemen who smoke in several counties in Virginia are
A dismissed immediately if caught.
B given notice of termination of contract.
C less likely to receive a disability pension.
D prevented from receiving a disability pension.

26 What is the purpose of the third paragraph on page 146?
A It summarises anti-smoking legislation.
B It demonstrates the writers' confidence in the anti-smoking programme of the U.S. Public Health Service.
C It demonstrates the success of the 18 reports issued by the Surgeons General.
D It summarises the success of the writer as Surgeon General.

27 In the paragraph headed 'Non smokers' Rights' on page 146, Phase 3
A extends the policies contained in Phases 1 and 2.
B justifies the trends in Phases 1 and 2.
C applies the policies contained in Phases 1 and 2.
D develops the trends begun in Phases 1 and 2.

Section 2 Writing

Question 1

Refer to Extract A on page 145.

a By means of a flow chart show the various stages in the introduction of anti-smoking legislation.
Refer to Extract B on page 146.

b Tabulate the anti-smoking policies which are accompanied by an explanation of the effect they will have on smokers.

Question 2

You must choose one of the titles below and write at least 60 of your own words. Remember: do not copy sentences from the article.

Either Study the table on page 144 and compare the relative success of the anti-smoking policies in the Asian countries mentioned.

Or The article on page 134 suggests a number of ways of measuring health. Based on your own knowledge and opinions, select the three you consider most important in your own country and rank them. Give reasons to account for your choice.

UNIT 8 · *What's it all for?*

INTRODUCTION

Independent learning
As the last Unit of the book, this is the least guided of all. Students are expected to apply many of the skills and techniques they have been introduced to in earlier Units. Students are now given even more autonomy in deciding how to organise their work, and indeed, in determining what direction this work takes.

If the book has been worked through systematically, this Unit will demonstrate the level of independent learning that students have reached. Therefore little extra guidance should be necessary.

If, on the other hand, the Unit is being taken out of sequence, then more guidance will probably be necessary. The exercises and ideas that follow here provide this.

The changing face of education
Everybody has some views on education. The theme is relevant to all students, whatever their disciplines.

Here we look at particular views on the topic and consider some new directions that education is taking.

Are we just interested in teaching knowledge and facts? What place do morals have in education? What and whose values do we teach? Just what kind of people are our education systems trying to produce? What kind of a world are we creating with our education systems? How is education changing to take account of technological developments?

These are just some of the issues that this Unit raises. It is left up to the students to express their ideas on such topical points.

OBJECTIVES OF THIS UNIT

Here we are mainly concerned with three things:

1 Teaching students to communicate ideas in an accurate and appropriate way in spoken and written form.
2 Encouraging students to put into practice the range of active and passive language skills taught and practised in this book.
3 Giving students practice in compiling a report as a member of a group.

A more precise list of skills taught and practised in this Unit is given below, section by section.

SECTION 1 — *SUMMARY*

In this section students will:

– practise putting their views in formal and informal discussion.

- practise skimming a text for precise information.
- practise devising and putting questions to obtain specific information.
- practise presenting the results of a survey in note and report form.
- practise comparing two reports for areas of similarity and difference.

The pictures and captions on page 000 are intended to lead students to the idea that different people have very different motives for continuing in education. This idea is carried on throughout the Unit.

Teaching tips

Page 151

A1 Before asking students to consider these questions, you could start off by asking students which person in the pictures they identify with most (or least).

A2 Students should work in groups for this discussion.

Suggest that they choose a chairperson to lead the discussion and to be responsible for reporting back to the whole class at the end.

Page 152

B The following list of names and terms appears in the text 'Yuppie Puppies'. *Sixth-formers* are pupils in their final two years at secondary school, usually aged between 16–18 years.

The National Curriculum refers to a proposal by the British government to impose a standard curriculum on all schools.

Socrates was an ancient Greek philosopher.

Oscar Wilde was an Irish playwright (1854–1900), well-known for his wit and humour.

Martin Luther King was an American civil rights leader who received the 1964 Nobel Peace Prize for his leadership of the non-violent struggle for racial equality in the US. He was assassinated in 1968.

Richard Branson is a successful businessman, owner of Virgin Records, well-known for his publicity-seeking projects *e.g.* hot-air ballooning, powerboat racing.

Yuppies stands for 'young, upwardly-mobile professionals' and refers to young people who are very involved in their professional careers and who are associated with smart living and expensive taste.

Yuppie Puppies are students who are likely to turn into Yuppies when they start work.

Page 152

B1 The following exercise could be done after the students have completed **B1*b***. It would serve to consolidate the question-making practice and also to introduce the idea of lead-in and follow-up questions.

While we are mainly concerned here with composing precise questions for a survey, it is also necessary for students to be aware that when questions of such a precise nature are put orally, the interviewer usually leads in gently. If we were to put questions bluntly without a softening introduction, the interviewee might at times be shocked by our abruptness. The exercise that follows helps students pose such questions in an appropriate fashion.

Supplementary exercise

Rearrange the introductory questions in column A below, to match the precise questions in column B.

	Column A		Column B
1	How do you view authority?	*A*	What social class do you feel you belong to?
2	Are you interested in politics?	*B*	Do you think that the people should be involved in decision-making?
3	How do you feel about religion?	*C*	Do you think your lifestyle will be the same as that of your parents?
4	What about the idea of central government?	*D*	Who are yours?
5	How do you see yourself?	*E*	Exactly what qualities do you need to possess to get on?
6	What about equality of the sexes?	*F*	For instance, what do you think of the police?
7	Do you believe in heroes?	*G*	Is it fair to all?
8	How do you feel about the legal system in your country?	*H*	Do you think that you have any influence on government decision-making
9	What kind of an effect is AIDS going to have on society?	*I*	Do you believe in God and an after-life? Do you practice your religion?
10	How do you see your future?	*J*	Do you think that there are any jobs that only men or only women can do?
11	What kind of people succeed in life?	*K*	Do you think that this disease will change people's behaviour?

Answers

1 *F* **2** *B* **3** *I* **4** *H* **5** *A* **6** *J* **7** *D* **8** *G* **9** *K* **10** *C* **11** *E*

Page 153

B2 You may need to refer students back to Unit 2 pages 21–23 for guidance on conducting a survey.

When deciding on the questions that they will ask, students should be encouraged to draw on those that they have inferred from the text.

Note, however, that some of these questions are on areas that may be considered rather sensitive, and it may be better to leave these out.

Page 153

B3 Here students will get intensive practise in asking questions.

It will probably be easiest for students to present the results of the survey in table or chart form.

B4 Before students write their report, ask them to look again at the text on page 152 and to analyse the structure of the report there.

Ask students to compare their analysis with this breakdown.

Analysis of report on survey

1 Introductory paragraphs

Describe the organisational details of survey

- where the survey was held
- the general topics that were covered.
- who the subjects of the survey were
- whether they represented a cross-section or not
- who the presenters were

2 The body of the report

1 or 2 questions per paragraph

- how the majority answered
- any important/interesting exceptions.

3 Concluding paragraph

A summary of what the survey tells us about the attitudes examined.

Ask students to plan their report in groups in a similar way. You may decide to ask students to write up the report individually or in groups.

Page 154

C1 Note that this exercise asks students to compare the results of the surveys, and not the form of the reports.

C1 *a* To facilitate comparison of the outcome of the British survey and of the survey conducted by your class, suggest that students draw up a chart to summarise the main similarities and differences.

Encourage students to identify all of the main topic areas common to the British survey and their own survey.

Have students fill in the chart in note form, considering general attitudes rather than exceptions.

Page 154

C2 These discussion points are quite important as they prepare students for the tasks which follow.

Ask students to prepare their responses to these questions in pairs.

Then put students into groups, with a chairperson, to discuss with others.

SECTION 2 – *SUMMARY*

In this section students will:

- practise reading and listening to pick out main points and attitudes.
- practise picking out specific information from a text and noting it in an appropriate way.
- practise using notes to give short talks.
- practise listening to a discussion involving more than two speakers to identify their position on an issue.
- learn useful discussion techniques *e.g.* interrupting, changing the direction of a discussion, agreeing and disagreeing in a formal and informal way.
- practise taking part in a formal discussion.
- practise writing an essay giving an opinion.

Teaching tips

Page 154

A1 Students should work individually at first and decide on their own what are the main aims of the education system described in their text.

Give them a limited time in which to do this.

Students working on the same text should be put together and asked to agree on the main aims.

Finally, ask them to compare their answers with the key. They should be able to discuss and account for any discrepancies.

Page 154

A2 Make it clear to students that they should report according to the guidelines, and not try to include everything in the text.

You may decide to ask students to work in groups all the time for this exercise. Or you may ask students to prepare notes individually and then compare them with others.

Page 155

A4*a* You may like to offer students more guidance in the designing of this table.

The students could use the guidelines suggested in **A2** as the criteria for the table; *i.e.* aims of the system
means of achieving the aims
problems.

Page 155

A4*b*/*c* Remind students that when filling in a table they should condense information. This will involve using key words where possible and not full sentences.

Pages 155–159

The texts in this section are exploited in the Students' Book for 'author's intention and main points'.

The teacher may also wish to focus on some of the vocabulary; the exercises which follow offer an opportunity to further develop the skill of guessing meaning from context.

The teacher might want to look at pages 91–92 in Unit 5 where some advice on this technique is given.

Page 155

Supplementary exercise — Text 1

The words and phrases listed below in the left-hand column are drawn from the text.
Among the phrases listed in the right-hand column you will find meanings for each of these words, in jumbled order.

For each focus word from the text, using any clues you can find, decide which meaning best matches it.
To make reference easier, you are given the position of the focus word in the text. For numbers 15–19 there will be 5 meanings with no focus words listed. Using the position reference, soon the text to locate appropriate words to match these.

Focus words	Position Col/Para		Meanings
1 cultural illiteracy	(in title)		*A* work done gladly
2 cite	1	3	*B* representatives of particular tribes, races or nations
3 bat an eye	1	4	*C* lack of
4 culled from	3	9	*D* quote or list
5 shibboleths	3	10	*E* incapable of carrying out their work properly
6 inept	3	11	*F* in an active or lively way
7 steeped in	1	13	*G* taken out of
8 a mixed blessing	1	16	*H* of poor quality
9 endorsement	1	16	*I* a lack of the basic knowledge that people need to be informed citizens
10 pertain to	1	17	*J* are connected with
11 trouble-shooter	2	18	*K* collection
12 animatedly	2	18	*L* show surprise
13 a labor of love	3	24	*M* an old and meaningless belief
14 superficiality	3	26	*N* no matter what
15 ...	1	3	*O* filled with
16 ...	3	8	*P* support for or approval of something
17 ...	3	9	*Q* someone who discovers and removes causes of problems
18 ...	3	23	*R* shallowness
19 ...	1	14	*S* something which brings both good and bad things

Answers

1*I* **2***D* **3***L* **4***G* **5***M* **6***E* **7***O* **8***S* **9***P* **10/11***Q* **12***F* **13***A* **14***R*

Answers

15*C* deficiency in, **16***H* crummy, **17***K* compilation, **18***N* regardless of, **19***B* ethnic groups

Page 157

It is important that students realise how much the context can help them to find out the meaning of difficult or unfamiliar words. The exercise that follows should promote this by forcing students to rely on the immediate context of the sentence for an indication of meaning.

Supplementary exercise — Text 2

Without referring to the text, complete the following sentences. You can use more than one word in each case.

1 It is easy to see how highly education is ____________ in Singapore.
2 Students ____________ their books with extraordinary diligence.

3 The government has no ____________ proclaiming that the brightest are the best.
4 Next month a pilot scheme is being ____________.
5 It has the catchy ____________, WISE, for 'worker improvement through secondary education'.
6 And a fiercely ____________ system, in which streaming begins at the age of nine, discourages some of the less able.
7 The government fears that Singapore's high tech ambitions will ____________ unless its education standard improves.
8 A committee pointed out that in another East Asian ____________, only 45% of the workforce lacked secondary education.
9 Things are similar at the top of the educational ____________.
10 Singapore's falling ____________ means that in the year 2000 its workforce will be increasing by only 1% a year.
11 The government ____________ that by 1995 a fifth of the workforce should be in professional or technical jobs.
12 Identifying the problem and ____________ it are, of course, two different things.

Compare the words and phrases that you have suggested with those of other students.

Make sure that the words you have chosen fit the context and fit grammatically into these sentences.

In some cases sentence clues will not have been sufficient to guess a precise meaning.

Look back at the paragraphs in which the sentences occur in Text 2 to check that the words you have suggested fit the overall meaning of the passage.

Page 158
The concepts of morals and values are central to this text. Understanding what they are and differentiating between them is vital if students are to be able to grasp the main points. The exercise which follows is designed to help them do this.

Supplementary exercise — Text 3

1 *a* Pick out from the first two paragraphs of the text the four moral issues mentioned.
b Do you think that students should discuss issues like these in school?
c Are there any other moral issues that deserve attention?

2 *a* From the remainder of the text, pick out the values that students might learn about in a values education class.
b Different people have different opinions on which values are most important.
Rearrange the list of values so that the ones which are most important to you are at the top.
c Would you add any other values to this list?
d Is the class in agreement on the order of the list?

Suggested answers

1 *a* euthanasia, hit and run accidents, abortion, teen pregnancies

2 *a* compassion, courtesy, honesty, tolerance, fairness, discipline, responsibility, sense of community

Page 159

When students read a text which contains a considerable number of unfamiliar words there is always a danger that their comprehension of the main points will be impeded.

This sometimes happens, not just because the text is difficult but because students fail to spot the relationships between words in the text. Thus they miss valuable clues to meaning.

The exercise which follows aims to sensitise students to such clues as synonomy (another word with a similar meaning), hyponomy (another word of the same area of meaning) and antonomy (a word of opposite meaning).

Supplementary exercise — Text 4

Refer to the text and answer the following questions.

1 In the first two paragraphs, find two phrases which mean the same as 'the fundamental aim'.
2 In the second paragraph there are a number of terms which mean 'free'. What are they?
3 In the first five paragraphs the ideas of 'freedom' and 'lack of freedom' arise often. Read through these paragraphs again and note down the words and phrases associated with the two ideas.
4 Throughout the whole text the idea of 'education and development' is central. In some instances the writer talks about this in a positive way, but at times he refers to its negative aspects.
   In two separate lists, note down the positive and negative phrases.

Page 160

B1 It should only be necessary to play the first five exchanges of this conversation to give students sufficient clues for this question.

Stop the tape at * and check if the positions of the three speakers have been understood.

If they have not, replay the first part of the conversation and stop the tape at tell-tale phrases such as:

S James . . . we're really most concerned with the idea of improving the present system . . .
. . . we're investing more and more money in education . . .
A Fox . . . a system that's far from satisfactory . . .
. . . the type of system you're supporting is, well, elitist . . .

Page 160

B2 If the teacher wishes to focus more closely on the way in which speakers interact, the following supplementary exercise could follow on from exercise **B2**.

The teacher could stop the tape at each letter in the tapescript and ask students to listen and decide what functions are being fulfilled.

The answers are marked on the tapescript for the convenience of the teacher.

Supplementary exercise

Consider the list of functions below.

Now listen to the conversation once more and decide when any one of these functions is being fulfilled.

Indicate to the teacher, and suggest which function you feel it is.

A finishing a point and stopping for a reply
B speaking in a continuous flow to prevent interruption
C introducing a new topic
D making use of a natural break in speech to come in
E appealing to the reason of others to make them agree
F taking up a point by coming in quickly and using a louder voice
G stopping interruptions by apologising and asking to be allowed to finish
H interrupting or taking up a topic by agreeing
I picking up a point made by another speaker
J disagreeing firmly
K promising to return to a point and continuing with another
L rephrasing what another speaker says in a more extreme way
M bringing the conversation back to the original topic
N posing a direct question

Page 160

C1 The teacher may feel that it is necessary to encourage students to examine some of Russell's arguments more closely to prepare for the discussion in exercise **C2**.

The supplementary exercise which follows focuses students' attention on important points within the text and requires them to use the context in order to understand these.

Supplementary exercise

With reference to the text, decide whether the statements below are true or false.

The answers are given in brackets for the convenience of the teacher.

A Russell feels that the value of education is sometimes questionable, since it does not always do what it aims to do. (F)
B Russell feels that we cannot ignore the opinion held by some people, that education is not necessarily desirable. (T)
C Opinions on what the aims of education should be are numerous and sometimes controversial. (T)
D According to Russell, the main debate on the purpose of education is between those who feel that we should be educated for wealth and those who feel that we should be educated for welfare. (F)

E An educated individual is guaranteed to be a valuable citizen. (F)

F Goethe's contribution to mankind has benefitted people from all societies. (F: Goethe was a nineteenth century German writer and thinker, while Watt was an inventor)

G A well-educated individual is likely to be a good citizen. But someone educated as a citizen is not necessarily a well-developed individual. (T)

H It is necessary to compromise between the two styles of education in order to produce a stable civilisation. (T)

I Russell stresses the need for the well-educated national citizen. (F)

J Russell is willing to sacrifice some of the finer aspects of education for the individual in order to produce a better world citizen.

In each case ask students to refer to the text and pick out the sentence or section which proves the answer is true, or supplies the correct answer.

Page 161

C2 *a/b* For this discussion have students agree on timing for preparation, discussion and summaries.

Stick to the agreed times as closely as possible.

Remind students to refer to the texts covered so far in the unit for ideas, and to the language learnt on page 160 for discussion techniques.

The teacher should move between groups during the preparation and discussion, and note down examples of the use of this language.

Page 161

C2 *c* The spoken summaries should be brief and should include the shared views of the group and any disputed points.

C3 For guidance on writing an argumentative essay, refer to the supplementary exercise on page 109 of the Teacher's Book.

SECTION 3 – *SUMMARY*

In this section we take a look at a recent development in the world of education and work, namely the increasing importance of information technology.

The texts and exercises here provide us with broad and thought-provoking views on the applications of this new technology.

Here students will learn to compile a report by:

- skimming available materials to find relevant sections.
- organising group tasks to share the work load.
- scanning texts for relevant information.
- reporting back to a group.
- collating ideas supplied by others.
- drawing up a plan for a report.
- following a plan to write sections of the report.
- putting together sections of the report in a cohesive and coherent way.

Teaching tips

Page 161

A Direct the students' attention to the visual at the top of page 162, while they are considering these four questions. This advertisement shows that IT refers to the use of computers.

B It might be a good idea for the teacher to briefly discuss the kind of reports that are likely to result from this activity. The teacher can adjust report length and the time to be spent on the activity, according to the needs of the students.

Page 163

B6 As suggested in this exercise, it is a good idea to have students look at each other's reports and evaluate them.

If students need guidance on the writing or evaluation of the reports, refer them to Unit 7, section 2 **D** on page 137 of the Students' Book.

When evaluating the reports, the main things the teacher should keep in mind are:

- the logical nature of the argument.
- the coherent and cohesive nature of the writing.

SECTION 4 – *SUMMARY*

In this section students will be involved in:

- conducting discussion for planning purposes.
- making presentations of a plan.
- holding a formal discussion to decide the merits and weaknesses of a plan.
- writing a report to compare two different plans.

Teaching tips

Page 178

A1 The class should select one member to control the discussion and act as chairperson. This could be the teacher but, on the other hand, the task would provide useful group management practice for one of the students.

Page 178

A2 The reason that it is suggested that the class should split into two or three groups only is to limit the number of presentations to be made.

In the case of a very large class, a greater number of groups could be formed. But then the presentation time would have to be rigidly controlled.

It should also be suggested to groups that they organise themselves by electing a chairperson and a secretary.

Page 178

A3 The most effective way of organising this exercise would be to split up the tasks between the group members.

For instance, if the talk can be divided into four sections, each member might prepare one.

A4 The presentation could be made by one member of each group, or it could be jointly presented with each speaker taking his/her turn, and one speaker summing up.

B1 Students may decide to amalgamate some groups at this stage to form a more unified front.

The teacher could encourage this by watching out for closeness of ideas between groups and suggesting such approaches.

B2 This should be a formal discussion, and again the teacher might call on a student to chair it.

The teacher could ask for comments on the chairing of the discussion at the end, stressing the strong points of the chairperson.

Page 179

C Have students note down the main features of the newly designed educational establishment.

Then have students note down the main features of the establishment they are actually studying in, using the same criteria.

Once these lists have been agreed and noted on the blackboard, all students have a good basis for the comparison report.

Emphasise that this report should be done individually and be brief.

SECTION 5 – *SUMMARY*

While this is a consolidation activity, based on interview work which students practised in this Unit, it is also an important practice activity for interview techniques. Here students will prepare for interview situations, such as for places of study, English exams or jobs.

In this section students will give consideration to:

- the areas that they are likely to have to talk about in an interview.
- the format of the interview.
- the qualities and strengths the interviewer will be looking for.
- the questions that may be asked.
- the information they need to have to answer such questions.

Here students will practise:

- composing the questions and answers predicted.
- answering questions under pressure.
- evaluating answers according to an agreed set of desirable qualities.

TEST PRACTICE

STUDY SKILLS

The questions which follow all refer to texts in Unit 8 of the Students' Book. You should read quickly through each text before answering the questions on it. If you do these 25 questions as a test, they should take you no longer than 35 minutes.

Part 1 Growing up with computers page 164

1 The writer's intention in the first paragraph is to
A look at some divisions in the population of the world.
B introduce a comparison of people's attitudes to computers.
C suggest that we cannot categorise people.
D state his opinion about computers.

2 In paragraphs 2 and 3, the writer shows his admiration for
A technophobes.
B technophiles.
C both technophobes and technophiles.
D neither technophiles nor technophobes.

3 What is the purpose of the sentence 'But what about the young?' in paragraph 4?
A It contradicts the writer's ideas in paragraphs 1, 2 and 3.
B It introduces the writer's main concern in the article.
C It reinforces the ideas expressed in paragraphs 1–3.
D It justifies the main point of paragraph 3.

4 The writer suggests that young people's attitudes to computers might be different to those of their parents because
A young people are generally better educated.
B there are computers in every home.
C computers form a part of all education programmes.
D young people are familiar with computers from an early age.

5 What is the relationship between the figures given in paragraph 7 and those in paragraph 8?
A The figures in paragraph 8 reinforce those in paragraph 7.
B The figures in paragraph 8 contradict those in paragraph 7.
C The figures in paragraph 8 justify those in paragraph 7.
D The figures in paragraph 8 contrast with those in paragraph 7.

6 The word 'though' in paragraph 9, line 90, is used to
A contradict ideas in the first part of the sentence.
B introduce a redefinition of the ideas in the first part of the sentence.
C introduce a logical consequence after the first part of the sentence.
D introduce an example to illustrate the point made in the first part of the sentence.

7 In paragraph 10 the author suggests that
A inhabitants of technological societies like technology more than other people.

B inhabitants of non-technological societies like technology more than others.
C industrialists do not like environmentalists.
D people's attitudes to technology are the same all over the world.

8 The last paragraph suggests that
A young people's attitude to technology is different to that of older people.
B young people's attitude to technology is comparable with that of older people.
C there is no point in comparing the attitudes of the young and the old to computers.
D young people have learned to fear computers.

Part 2 Computer science page 167

9 According to the article, what is the outlook for the development of computers in the future?
A It has reached a peak.
B It seems to be on the decline.
C It is clearly in a trough at the moment.
D It is likely to be sustained.

10 How many elements are included in the study of computer science, according to the text?
A 1
B 2
C 3
D 4

11 The EAPS and MAPS courses differ
A in a fundamental way.
B in terms of emphasis.
C in the name only.
D in their overall aims.

12 The paragraph entitled 'Entrance Requirements'
A suggests that students with one 'A' Level pass in any branch of Maths stand a reasonable chance of being accepted on the course.
B is a formal statement of the general entrance requirements for the university.
C only offers guidance to future students of Computer Science interested in hardware.
D only courses where the emphasis is on software do not need two science 'A' Levels.

13 In the paragraph entitled 'Facilities', the word 'Additionally' in line 0 refers to
A the various computer systems which students may use.
B the courses that the students may take part in at the university Computing Centre.
C the other students who are studying on different but related courses throughout the university.
D the hardware courses that may be attended as an alternative to software courses.

14 The last paragraph, 'Careers in Computer Science', encourages students to apply for the courses on offer at Sussex because
A the course at Sussex is far more varied than those at other universities.
B the university is eagerly seeking skilled staff in this area and needs new trainees.
C the jobs for such graduates are growing in number.
D they will be prepared to do all kinds of work no matter what skills are necessary.

Part 3 All for IT page 168

15 Which of the following statements best sums up the opening sentence?
A As yet the authorities have not recognised the importance of IT in education.
B Up to now computing has received more attention than IT, but that is changing.
C The authorities mistakenly believe that IT is more important than computing.
D Computing has replaced IT in the school curriculum.

16 The author maintains that
A the majority of educationalists eagerly await the introduction of IT.
B there is resistance to the introduction of IT in schools.
C people are suspicious of IT in education.
D educationalists do not understand the importance of IT.

17 The word 'this' in paragraph 4 refers to
A the national core curriculum.
B a knowledge of IT.
C a knowledge of computing.
D educational centres.

18 Low argues that
A people should be familiar with the world of IT.
B people should not become involved in computer programming.
C people should know exactly how a computer works.
D people should not be able to use high tech.

General questions

For these questions you will need to look again through the texts on pages 164–168 Unit 8.

19 Which text lays the least stress on IT, and is more concerned with computing?
A Growing Up With Computers
B Computer Science
C All for IT
D None of these

20 Which text takes an objective stand on the subject of computer technology?
A Growing Up With Computers
B Computer Science

C All for IT
D None of these

Part 4 Index page 171

22 The name of a group should give you some idea of what it contains. But with some systems you can set up a short description to help identify the text.
Information on this can be found on
A page 167
B page 538
C page 107
D page 181

23 How many different pages are referred to under the entry Headers and Footers?
A 1
B 3
C 5
D 4

Part 5 Bibliography: Sources of Additional Information page 172

24 Which of the following publications would be of most use to foreign students going to study at undergraduate level in the UK?
A Scholarships Guide for Commonwealth Postgraduate Students
B Degree Course Guides
C Awards for Commonwealth University Academic Staff
D SSRC/Handbook Studentships

25 Which of the following publications is most likely to be of interest to foreign postgraduate students?
A Research Fields in Physics at UK Universities and Polytechnics
B TEFL/TESL Academic Courses in the UK
C SSRC/Handbook Studentships
D Financial Aid for First Degree Study at Commonwealth Universities

succession, so that individual students are called on to answer, while the other students listen and assess.

Alternatively, the questions can be distributed to the students, who can then conduct mock interviews in groups or pairs.

A Personal questions

- Where do you come from?
- Tell me something about your hometown.
- Is there anything special about it?
- What do people there generally do for a living?
- Would you recommend your hometown to tourists?
- Do you come from a large family?
- Where do you come in the family?
- What do you imagine your family is doing at this moment?
- How do you spend your free time at home?
- If your sources were unlimited and you had as much free time as you wanted, what would you do?
- Have you read any good books lately – or seen any good films?
- What did you do during the last holidays?
- Tell me something about your present studies.
- What aspects of this educational establishment do you like/dislike?

B Text related questions

Note: All these questions relate to the texts in Unit 8.

- Which of the texts would you read if you were thinking of studying computing?
- What do you think the illustration on page 163 represents?
- In the text 'Growing Up With Computers' on page 164 we learn that people have different attitudes to computers.
  Which of the categories mentioned do you think you belong to? Why?
- The texts suggest that not being able to handle computers is a severe disadvantage these days. Do you agree?
- Which of the views on education described in the texts on pages 155–159 would you identify with most?
- What do you understand by the phrase 'Yuppie puppie'?
- Do you think that the advertisement on page 169 is an effective one? Why?

C Studies/career

- Where will you go from here?
- How do you see your future academic career?
- What do you imagine you will be doing in ten years time?
- What is your parents' attitude to your future plans?
- What factors influence you when you are making future plans?
- Why is English important to you?

TAPESCRIPTS

UNIT 1 *Help yourself*

Part 1 Listening Extracts

Extract 1

It must be understood that peanut shelling alone demands an enormous amount of time. Before sowing the pods must be opened to remove the peanuts which are then placed in the ground. After harvesting, the pods must be detached from the stem, then opened in order to harvest the peanuts destined for sale or the next sowing.

Extract 2

The stove automatically suits women's cooking requirements because they themselves build it to fit whatever pot they wish to use it for. Construction is so simple that many women make two or more to fit different sizes of pot. First, the women position three stones on the ground, with the chosen pot resting on them. Then they build a low cylinder of clay around the stones, leaving a small gap around the pot for smoke to côme out. After it has dried a little, the women cut a semi-circular hole in the wall so that they can insert wood.

Extract 3

One view on why the rate of development is slow is the 'vicious circle' argument. This suggests that poverty results in low investment; in turn, low investment results in low production, low production in low income, and low income in poverty. There are other vicious circles, too. Hunger results in poor physique which in turn leads to low production. A third circle is that of poverty leading to low demand and hence low production. All three circles occur simultaneously and interact.

Part 2 Housing the Poor — An Interview

Q: . . . and so the fundamental question is 'how can the poor gain access to decent shelter?' Isn't it the case that whether we consider rural areas or urban areas, large or small, the majority of the world's population seems condemned to substandard shelter conditions?

A: I'm afraid there's a great deal of truth in what you say. It was hoped that population distribution policies would help to solve this problem.

Q: You mean you'd expected that lower population densities would result in better living conditions generally?

A: That's right and they've failed and the problem remains as there's no correlation between city size and accessibility to shelter and services.

Q: So if what we might term 'appropriate' distribution policies can't solve the low-income shelter problem, what approach are you adopting now?

A: Okay – we have to look elsewhere for a lead, look at our own experience; what has that taught us? How can we apply the lessons we've learnt? Can any of the principles – established, mind you, in one specific case – be adapted, broadened, generalized and have validity in all situations? That's the question *we*'ve been researching and there do appear to be three common factors. Firstly, understanding the nature of the problem. Now on a smallscale, ad-hoc and self-help solutions and that sort of thing have in many cases dealt with a localized problem admirably. But they can't deal with the over-riding problem which is the problem of scale.

Q: But there are examples of fairly large-scale schemes where what you call the ad-hoc, self-help approach *has* worked ... while, incidentally, a parallel 'top-down' approach has had much less success or even failed.

A: These success stories get written about but they're not common; and we're talking about a *huge* problem here.

Q: Another suggestion being made is the need to involve the private sector. How would you view that sort of involvement?

A: Yes, but the private sector's obliged to do what's profitable, not what's needed. And the poor in search of shelter are *not* a lucrative market. In fact, it's becoming clear to us that the actual reason for the problem is that societies in developing countries accept the very problem itself as normal.

Q: The poor accept poor shelter and the privileged accept that the poor live in these conditions?

A: Well, yes, that's it ...

Q: So what does understanding the problem mean for you?

A: The vastness of the problem requires massive, nationwide efforts and huge investment – it's not something which can be effectively dealt with by small administrative or bureaucratic concessions, nor is it a target for gimmicks and informal solutions.
The second factor, incidentally, follows directly from this and we'd call it political commitment. Now, housing the poor isn't in itself a particularly important vote-winning method; those who lack shelter usually lack political clout. But there are cases where national shelter policies have been launched and implemented in response to widely-felt needs and as the centrepiece of a high level political strategy.

Q: But if you do this, what about addressing the actual, *real* needs of the poor?

A: Well, this is obviously our major concern ...

Q: Yes, but one feels a lack of, let's call it 'consultation', with the people actually involved ...

A: Ah, but to push it through, get it working, you have to get the political wheels in motion. And *then* you've got the third factor, the adoption of clear national policies with definite and achievable targets. And this is where account would be taken of what the people say, in defining those targets. But you must note the word 'achievable'; this *has to* temper public comment again because of the scale involved. Of course we ask, of course we listen, of course this feedback helps to mould our decisions, but do realise the sheer size and complexity of the machinery involved – the public offices, ministries, planning departments, banks.
If you accept that a national housing policy is going to change things for most people quickest then you have to accept that a good deal of decision-making will be, so to speak, *imposed*.

UNIT 2 *Join the club*

A: Against a background of football violence culminating in the Heysel stadium disaster in 1985 and also the Bradford fire in the same year, the Popplewell Committee recommended (erm) membership of football clubs be made compulsory and the British Government has decided to implement (-ment) a plan to make membership of English football clubs compulsory for all fans. Dr. Foster, do you think such membership schemes will actually solve the problem of violence at football matches?

B: I believe so but you've got to realise first that these, er, membership schemes have not been fully implemented. Initially, the Government did want 100% membership scheme, but now they've settled for a point where membership is only essential for 50% of a club's supporters, that's to say, the other 50% of the ground people can just come in and pay on the day. It's only one club, Luton Town, that have implemented a system where there's been a complete ban on away supporters; that is to say that the membership is 100% for home supporters only.

A: But this ban on (a-) away fans, isn't this going to give (erm) the home team an unfair advantage during during the match, in that there's no away support?

B: Undoubtedly that's the case but we've got to consider also that the football world is not the world as a whole. We've got to think of not only what is good for football but what is good for the community and quite honestly people who've got no interest in football are sick and tired of violence and damage being committed to their property and to themselves every time there's a football match in a big town. It just can't go on any more.

A: But what actually is to stop a hooligan from joining such a scheme and then the violence continuing, only with (um with) members committing the violence?

B: Well, we institute a system of (a) scrutinising the membership and then, because that supporter will have a computerised membership card,something like a credit card with their number, as soon as they commit any offence at all, we would be able to withdraw their membership and they'll never be able to come into the ground again; this kind of control just doesn't exist at the moment.

A: I see. (Er) What actually have been the effects of the membership scheme as it's been introduced so far? Has it been successful?

B: Well, certainly (in) in – if the Luton case is considered it's been very successful (um) there's been a complete absence of violence at the ground, the number of police required is much safer, before when a visiting – an away team came to Luton, escorting them from the railway station, through the main centre of the town and disturbing shoppers and thousands of people, who I again say do not go to football matches, these people are not being troubled, so yes, there has been a complete absence of violence inside and outside the ground.

A: How about the – the man in the street, the ordinary man in the street. Isn't such a scheme off-putting and, and intimidating (er) to him? Won't this stop (er) the genuine support from, from actually going to see the one-off game where he may not wish to, to become a member?

B: I think you've got to realise that membership of our scheme doesn't mean that you buy a series of tickets for the whole season's matches. It means you just pay a token sum of one pound and that entitles you to a year's membership. Then you can come and buy tickets and pay to get into as many or as few games as you like. So the only trouble initially is applying for the card and we do have very (err) many outlet points in the town where people can go into shops, businesses to apply for the membership, it can be issued from there and they're also allowed to pay of course to – for matches with credit cards as well, so what we're really doing is making it much easier for the genuine supporter to come and watch the game.

A: (Um) To what extent has this affected the gates? Do you find that (um) fewer supporters are now going to watch matches?

B: Well, you've got to bear in mind that Luton did have a large number of away supporters coming to the games especially from the London area but those extra supporters meant extra policing. Now, you could say that it's better to have the customers coming through the turnstiles and we would like more people to be watching the games, that's undeniable, but it's a fact of life and it's something that the club and the community have got to work about together. Quite honestly, Luton Town are prepared to have lower gates if it means that the people of Luton and not just the football supporters of Luton, can go about their business in safety on a Saturday afternoon. We're not just interested in football's point of view, we, along with the community, the police and the whole area, want to do something about this problem for all our sakes and not just for the football world's sake.

A: (Fi) Finally, can I – can I ask you, do you feel that (um) the implementation of membership schemes has, has been a success? Is this a solution? Are we going to see the end of football violence at English Clubs?

B: You've only got to look at the success of the Luton scheme to see the answer to that. Yes, I do think membership schemes can work and I just wish that the rest of the football world would not have such a 'head in the sand' attitude to it all and would realise that nowadays it's a minority sport. We've got to think about the society as a whole and football should not be so insular and inward-looking in its attitude.

A: Dr. Foster, thank you very much.

UNIT 3 *A question of power*

Part 1 The Problem of Energy

A: World energy consumption continues to grow. In developing countries it has been growing at a much faster rate than in the world as a whole. With the fluctuation of oil prices over the last 10 to 15 years, and more recent warnings of its limited supply, scientists have been looking into various alternative sources of energy. To talk about the range of energy sources, and some related problems, we have Alexandra Payne here in the studio with us.
Are we really facing an energy crisis?

B: We are definitely facing difficulties now, but it's hard to say when or even whether supplies will run out. There's little to be gained from speculating about exact dates, like saying we only have enough oil to last until the year 2020. It's better to develop clean safe alternatives now so that we always have options, if and when a real crisis should arise. *1

A: Well, what sources are we most dependent on at the moment to generate electricity?

B: I suppose the ones that most people would think of first are oil, coal and gas. We have depended on these for many years now. Add to that hydro-electricity schemes which also produce substantial amounts of electricity. And then recently there's been nuclear power. *2

A: On the question of nuclear power and nuclear energy, it's very much talked about in recent times, and especially the aspect of safety. Now do you think that there's a reason to stop, or to question the development of nuclear power for this reason?

B: I can only give a personal opinion. Er, there must be difficulties as we have seen evidence of near disasters at 3 mile island, Windscale, and, more recently, at Chernobyl. It's all very well, comparing percentage risk figures, for example, saying that nuclear power stations only cause so many deaths every 100 years, whereas road safety is more important, but the fact remains that nuclear accidents are potentially much more dange-rous than other ones. Add to that the risk of technological abuse – people manufacturing weapons with the technology – the restricted access to such a high technology means of energy production, what I mean is so that at present it's entirely controlled by a handful of countries, and very few people are employed in the industry, and I have to say that I favour the development of alternative power sources. *3

A: Well, in spite of all these disadvantages that you point out, as you know yourself many governments encourage the expansion of the nuclear sector. It must have great advantages over oil, coal and gas. Can you give us an idea of what they might be?

B: Yes, if the difficulties I have just mentioned can be overcome, then there are several. First of all, only a tiny amount of nuclear fuel is needed to produce very large amounts of energy. Secondly, after building it is cheap to run. That's building the plant, I mean. Fuel is readily transported. It's very compact. There is very little pollution whilst the plant is operating, and there's high efficiency in transferring the energy from the fuel to electricity. *4

A: Now these advantages clearly are great, and if governments continue to operate their present policies and go ahead with the expansion of nuclear power do you think that we can expect to be abandoning such sources as oil, coal and gas in the future, in favour of nuclear power?

B: Well, I think you have to bear in mind that there are still vast reserves of these fossil fuels under the earth, especially coal and new deposits are being discovered all the time. On the contrary, I think that we could see a return to more traditional forms of technology and the more efficient exploitation of these reserves. *5

A: Leaving aside nuclear power and the conventional sources for the moment, do we have other choices of energy sources, and if we do, what are they?

B: Yes, we have a lot of choice, for example, we have solar, geothermal wind, wave, tidal power, bio-mass and Ocean Thermal Energy Conversion, often shortened to OTEC. So, as you can see, the list is quite extensive. But then it's limited by financial considerations, as well as factors like public opinion, and geographical location. You can't go using solar energy in a place that has very little sun.

A: You talked about solar energy, you talk about tidal energy. We hear about them in the news, and we read about them. They are, I think, what they call the alternative energy sources. They are rather fashionable at the moment, aren't they? But are they realistic, realistic on a large scale? Can they provide us with a substantial part of our energy needs?

B: Well, I think it's difficult to generalise, but needs is the operative word. If energy is needed for domestic heating or lighting, then yes, small scale schemes can work well. But if it's needed for industry then they may not be efficient and cost effective. *6

Part 2 Nuclear Power

Presenter: The Layfield Report has just been published following a 3-year-long inquiry. It concerns the proposal to build a Pressurised Water Reactor (PWR as it is called) at Sizewell, which is situated on the southeast coast of England. As opposed to existing British reactors which use gas, the PWR-type of reactor uses water under high pressure to transfer the heat from the reactor core to the steamgenerating plant.

The great advantage of the PWR is that it's very compact. In fact, it's commonly used in nuclear submarines. Now, the problem is that people are worried about the safety aspects. The reactor involved in the Three-Mile Island accident was of this type but not of the same design as the one they want to build at Sizewell.

I asked Prof. Webster to come along and talk about the Sizewell reactor.

Peter Webster: We regard it as being safe. A great many safety features have been engineered into it. That means that if things start to go wrong the whole thing just closes down.

Now, if things do go wrong with a PWR – you don't have much time. Things go wrong very quickly – which means that the safety devices have to work very quickly. But you must remember that we now have 30 years' experience with this kind of reactor throughout the world. And we're pretty sure that the various safety devices work very efficiently.

Presenter: Now, we've had the Chernobyl disaster relatively recently, although it's a different sort of reactor. And there have been other nuclear accidents in the past. So, understandably, people are worried about safety, and particularly that the operators and technicians can make mistakes. To what extent can we guarantee that this sort of human error won't happen in a PWR?

Peter Webster: Well, there's no doubt that they are proof against it much more than the reactor that exploded at Chernobyl. There, the operators were able to override safety devices. Now that certainly can't happen with the PWR that is proposed for Sizewell.

On the other hand, in the PWR the operating fluid is water. In the Advanced Gas-cooled reactors (AGRs) that we have in this country, the operating fluid is Carbon Dioxide and there is a giant graphite core. Now, things can go wrong with AGRs just as they can with PWRs. But the difference is that things happen much more slowly in the AGR.

However, both are thought to be extremely safe.

Presenter: Are you suggesting, then, that people have nothing to worry about?

Peter Webster: Well, people shouldn't be unduly worried. You see, if you compare risks from other possible accidents I think you'll find that nuclear power stations are much less dangerous than, say, chemical factories. You hear of some really horrifying chemical accidents. At Bhopal, in India, for instance – that was a real tragedy, and over two thousand people were killed.

Presenter: Let's turn now to the economics of nuclear reactors. It has been said that the PWR is more cost efficient. Why is it reckoned to be more economical than, say, AGRs?

Peter Webster: Well, I think what people are really talking about when they say economical is capital costs. That is, the capital cost of building the power station, which you have to pay back over thirty years or so. The PWR gives the best payback.

Having said that, the Layfield Report now seems to suggest it is possible that the AGR might turn out to be cheaper, so that point isn't very clear.

But Layfield does state that either of these – the AGR or the PWR, will be cheaper than coal in terms of generating electricity. And that's in spite of the fact that the price of coal has fallen sharply over the last 3 years.

Presenter: I was talking there to Prof. Peter Webster.

UNIT 4 *Ringing the changes*

A Two Residents of Malacca

Speaker 1

In the old days / town has seen better days / port has silted up / volume of shipping has greatly decreased / port has become less and less important / warehouses have fallen into dacay / As the port silted up, foreign trade decreased / the town has diminished in importance as a trading centre / business has moved to Kuala Lumpur.

Speaker 2

Town has picked up wonderfully / It's not that long ago that many of the buildings were ramshackle / recently the skyline has changed dramatically / several new high rise have gone up / old buildings demolished to make way for new housing development / lot of land reclaimed / especially around port area / population has shot up / Malacca has become a busy business centre / industrial estates have mushroomed / economic emphasis has shifted away from the port area to new factories and businesses / tourist trade has taken over, especially in the old town.

Jyothi: Aiya, things have changed, you know, not like in the old days, town has seen better days.

Azmel: No. no, I don't agree with that. I think town has picked up a lot. You see, it's not that long ago that many of the buildings were ramshackle and falling down, but nowadays we got lot of new buildings and . . .

Jyothi: What new buildings?

Azmel: Recently, the skyline has changed a lot isn't it? Several new highrises have gone up, old buildings demolished to make way for new housing development and a lot of/lot of land claims[1], especially around port area.

Jyothi: Yeah, why? Because the port has become more and more silted up hmmm? All the port – no-one wants to go there anymore.

Azmel: No.

Jyothi: No ships come here anymore. Shipping has gone down a lot, you know. Hah, the port is becoming less and less important. The warehouses, all the warehouses there, all fallen into decay, no warehouses there anymore. Then as the port silted up, the foreign traders do not come anymore, you know.
Hah, foreigh trade has decreased; the town has diminished in importance as a trading centre, I tell you.

Azmel: But Malacca has become a busy business centre and industrial estates have grown up all over the place. Business has shifted away from the port area to new factories and businesses.

Jyothi: Yes, business has shifted to K.L.[2]

Azmel: But you must not forget this. Tourist trade has taken over especially in the old town.

1 land claims – reclaimed land
2 K.L. – Kuala Lumpur

Part 2 Overheating

A: Waste industrial gases are causing us more and more concern these days. And carbon dioxide in particular is causing us worries. We are discharging 10,000 million tons of CO2 a year from burning fuel. This makes CO2 the largest single waste product from our socicty.
I asked Professor Nicholas Park why he is concerned about this.

B: The main reason for concern is that carbon dioxide and some of the other gases are causing climatic change. The effect they cause is known as the Greenhouse Effect. Basically, what happens is these gases form a type of blanket that surrounds the earth. The heat is kept inside – and the thicker the blanket gets, the warmer it gets inside.
As the level of these gases in the atmosphere increases, the possibility of the world's climate changing increases. Now research has shown that in the last ice age there were about 200 parts of CO2 per million in the earth's atmosphere. At the start of the industrial revolution, there were 280 parts. The level now stands at 350, and it's still rising.
And without question by the end of this century we will cross the 600 mark.
So, in fact, we have accidentally changed the natural composition of the atmosphere.

A: You mentioned other gases apart from CO^2. What are they?

B: Well, we're not just concerned with carbon dioxide. The level of Methane has also risen – and this is probably connected with rice production, and also cattle raising. Methane is a more natural product and is produced in an agricultural environment. But, there are other gases produced in more industrial environments. For example, we have the chlorofluorocarbons. Now, these are gases which are not produced naturally. They are solely industrial products, and they stay in the atmosphere for a long time. Like CO2, they have an effect on climate. But they also have an additional effect in that they affect the ozone layer.

A: When were these chlorofluorocarbons first discovered?

B: During this century, when we started to produce things like fridges and aerosols.

In fact, these gases are used in a huge variety of ways.

A: Are you actually suggesting that if this situation is allowed to continue that we are going to significantly affect our survival on this planet?

B: I think it's almost inevitable that we will move the climate system outside the natural range. I fear this has started already.

A: Well, what could this mean, in real terms? How will we be affected?

B: Effects will vary from place to place. There will assuredly be winners or losers in the question of global climate change.
Our best guess would be that countries in the far north will, on the whole, benefit. But countries that are reasonably well off today might suffer.

A: Already some pressure groups are demanding that pollution controls should be tightened. And a number of initial measures have been taken.
Do you think there is any more that can be done to halt this problem?

B: There is no doubt that the scale of the problem that we are now facing is a truly global one. We can no longer depend on small-scale local initiatives to find a solution. This is an international problem, and if the scientists are to have any impact we need international co-operation. It is encouraging to see that the world scientific community has recognised this need, and is beginning to work more closely together.

Extracts

1. And without question by the end of this century we will cross the 600 mark.
2. I think it's almost inevitable that we will move the climate system outside the natural range.
3. **There will assuredly be winners or losers in the question of global climate change.**
4. Our best guess would be that countries in the far north will, on the whole, benefit.
5. But countries that are reasonably well off today might suffer.

UNIT 5 *Food for thought*

Discussing agricultural self-sufficiency

Mr. Bivina: I see commodity prices are down again.

Mr. Iddrisu: Yes, and it's not doing our economy in Lodos any good at all, I can tell you.

Mr. Bivina: Cocoa's your main crop, isn't it?

Mr. Iddrisu: That's right, over 80% of our exports in 1984, but things haven't been so good since then.

Mr. Bivina: Why's that?

Mr. Iddrisu: Well, we can never be sure of the price and because of that it is difficult to plan long term. For instance, in 1980 43% of our Gross Domestic Product in Lodos came from cocoa, but by 1984 it was down to 26.1%.

Mr. Bivina: And that's caused you to grow less cocoa, has it?

Mr. Iddrisu: Well, our farmers don't grow so much due to the variations in price.

B: . . . and as a result you must be encouraging them to grow other crops?

I : Well, actually we want them to go back into cocoa.

B: Now, what on earth is the reason for that?

I : Well, you see, as I said, the continued low prices meant that the farmers couldn't cover their costs, which is why many of them got out of cocoa production and, as a result of this, we must now invest a lot of capital in order to raise production totals. In fact, over the next few years we will be spending 23 1/2 million dollars to get the plantations working at full capacity again.

B: What's behind this policy?

I : Well, we hope to earn more foreign exchange by exporting more cocoa.

B: But surely you will be in the same old position as soon as the cocoa prices go down again?

I : Well, what else can we do?

B: Well, in the Cameroons we have encouraged farmers to produce more foodstuffs like maize, yams and potatoes and, as a result of this, we are now virtually self-sufficient in food.

I : Yes, but how do you earn foreign currency?

B: In fact, owing to this policy of self-sufficiency, we simply do not need to earn as much as we are able to provide for our own needs.

I : But of course in the Cameroons you have oil to boost your foreign currency earnings. We rely on cocoa exports to provide foreign exchange.

B: Well, yes, but you could always apply for aid during the changeover period.

B: But don't forget you have good contacts with Britain and France. Where can we look?

B: Why not try IFAD? That's where we got most help from and, as a result, there were no strings linking us to a particular country.

I : What's IFAD?

B: The United Nations International Fund for Agricultural Development. It specializes in helping poor farmers grow more food.

I : I suppose it's worth a try but what about technical expertise? The men in our country have always grown cocoa. It's all they know.

B: Well, financial rewards are the best incentive. As soon as they see it pays to switch, they will, especially if you are able to provide fertilizers and low cost technology.

I : I see, but why the turnaround? You used to export a lot at one time, didn't you?

B: Well, I suppose we're just tired of seeing our foreign currency reserves slipping away and decided to make a major policy review. After that, it was quite straightforward, especially with the technical help we received from the International Institute for Tropical Agriculture in Nigeria.

I : Well, you may have been convinced but how did you get the ordinary farmers on your side?

B: Quite simple. I put it down to women.

I : Women! But it is the men who grow cocoa.

B: Yes, but who grows the vegetables and maize? As soon as they saw the benefits and were able to feed, clothe and educate their children, then they were converted and consequently they started to influence their husbands.

I : But what happens if people still want to grow cocoa?

B: Well, that's the time to apply disincentives. Once you start to charge low prices for cocoa and the farmers realize their lack of income is due to growing cash crops they will soon change their ways.

I : You make it sound very easy but I think the obstacles we would have to overcome are greater than the ones you faced.

B: Well, it's up to you but don't think it's all about money; education and changing attitudes is what really counts, that's why it needs such careful planning.

I : I'm not entirely convinced yet. There are a lot of things that need to be thought about first.

UNIT 6 *A brave new world*

Part 1–5 Extracts

Extract 1

A: What is the advantage of biological catalysts?

B: Well, whereas with many chemical catalysts you have to work at high pressures – sometimes at hundreds of atmospheres, and at high temperatures – usually at hundreds of degrees centigrade, biological catalysts function in normal conditions. They'll work in water at standard pressures and temperatures.

A simple example of this is one we use every day – when we wash clothes. In the past we had to boil our clothes to get them clean. The old detergents only worked at high temperatures. But modern washing powders work at room temperature and the reason for this is that they contain biological catalysts. These catalysts eat fat, protein and carbohydrates off our clothes and things like that.

But another area where biological catalysts are very important is in degrading effluents. We use them to take the dangerous chemicals out of waste from factories, chemical forms, and so on. We also use them on drinking water – to purify it. Firms, of course benefit from this – as it costs less to get rid of their effluents. So they save money. And the country benefits, too – less waste around . . .

Extract 2

A: And what about virus resistance?

B: Well, virus resistance is really very impressive indeed. A lot of experiments have been done – a tremendous amount of research. Now, on the control plant which didn't get the engineered trial, you can see lesions of virus. But if we look at the other tobacco plant, the one that the cupoid protein gene has been implanted into – well, it's completely resistant to the lesion . . . doesn't get any at all.

A: Yes, it sounds very exciting. Now, is this going to change the face of agriculture? Will it have a big effect on things . . . as they stand . . . ?

B: Oh, I don't think that there is any doubt but that it will. And this would be marvellous for the farmer – the resistance is built into the seed. No more need for sprays!

He just puts the seed in the earth and it will grow up as a resistant plant, needing very little care.

Extract 3

A: What results have been achieved by this method? What sort of plants have been grown?

B: Well, first of all we used this technique with tobacco. This is one of the simplest plants to work with.

However, it has also been used with many crop plants like potatoes and tomatoes. And this has been very successful. Then, in more recent times it has been tried on oil seed rape, sugar beet and soya beans.

A: What's the advantage of having plants that are resistant to herbicides?

B: Well, it means that better herbicides can be used. Such herbicides would be easier on the environment, as they are easily degraded in the soil – biodegradable, we call it.

Now, these 'better' herbicides that we have at the moment usually don't have selectivity. They kill off the weed all right, – but they kill the crop, too.

If we put into the crop a protein that will resist the herbicide, then the crop will survive, and while the wheat or maize grows on, the weeds will be killed.

Extract 4

A: By putting genes into animals how can we help the farmer? For instance, can we make leaner beef . . . or . . . ?

B: Actually, there is some idea that we might be able to. A recent experiment was done on mice – and they put human growth hormones into these mice . . .

A: You mean, they put the gene in?

B: That's right, they put in the gene, and the result was dramatic. The mice grew as big as rats. This, of course, caused a great deal of fuss. The animal husbandry experiments are trying to get these genes into sheep and cattle . . . with limited success, I think.

Extract 5 A new vaccine is being launched in Britain to combat Hepatitis B. It is cheaper than existing vaccines and should halve the costs.

Hepatitis B attacks the liver, and if it isn't immediately deadly, it can cause cancer years later.

The virus is transmitted through body fluids and blood – and causes as many as a million deaths per year.
The existing vaccine – which is administered in three injections, is costly at about 60 sterling for the course. Smith, Kline and French have come up with Engerix-B, in their Belgian labs, and it only costs half of that amount. It is the first genetically engineered vaccine to be sold in Britain.

Part 2 — Plain Speaking

A: Let's move on now to an area that appears to be of great concern to you. I'm talking about the idea of taking a desirable characteristic from one plant and transferring it into another.
Well, this has actually been happening for thousands of years, hasn't it? And surely the new techniques are just speeding up the progress of plant and animal breeding that we've had for a long, long time.

B: Well, in one sense that's true, and in another sense, it isn't.
There is no doubt that genetic engineering saves us money and time in breeding. But, on the other hand, by employing this technique we run the risk of narrowing our genetic diversity. We're in the process of creating super-breeds with certain strains, and leaving other strains by the wayside.
We've started to narrow our genetic diversity in other ways. I'm thinking of how we have monocultured our plants and animals in agriculture.
Genetic engineering further exacerbates this situation by speeding up the monoculturing.
Now, this is different from traditional breeding. Of course man has always bred animals – but not in this way.
What men have ever carried out such outrageous experiments, as are being done now? For instance, take the growth hormone research. Scientists have taken human growth hormones and placed them in mice. Human hormones in mice! So what happened? Well, I'll tell you what happened – you had huge mice. Super-mice, we call them. Then they had babies and passed these hormones on. Now every generation of mice has human hormones. It's ridiculous – absurd.
There was another experiment: last year scientists took the gene that emits light in the firefly. They inserted it into a tobacco plant, and now . . . that plant lights up, day and night.
So this technology allows us to go beyond nature's limits. Now – technology is unrestrained. We can cross totally unrelated species and get . . . who knows what . . .!
Well, this creates serious environmental questions. Not only that – it creates grave ethical questions, too.

Part 3 — A Patent on Life

A: Following on the development of 'new' species of plants and animals – there is now the question of being able to patent these species. What do you find so objectionable about that?

B: The US patent office has decided that any animal on this planet can be patented! With the exception of man, that is. Well, what does this mean, exactly. It means that if you put a gene into an animal, you can claim that animal as your invention. Of course this is totally absurd. The patent office, has therefore reduced the whole biological kingdom to the status of a commodity – a manufactured good, like an electric toaster or a car.

In fact, they said living things are to be considered manufactured processes and compositions of matter.

A: Well, I would agree with you that the idea is rather absurd.

But, from a practical point of view – surely you must agree that if millions of dollars have been spent developing a particular variety of rabbit by a company or university – well, surely they are entitled to protect their investment in a legal way.

B: They are not entitled to take the common inheritance of this planet and turn it into private property. Horses, cows, sheep and goats – even mice, have been here for millions of years. They are no one's property. The idea of patenting them strains the bounds of rational thought.

And this trend will have dramatic implications for farmers. If this patenting goes ahead, and spreads to Europe it'll mean that farmers will have to buy patented animals from chemical companies – and pay royalties on their young.

And every time farmers want to sell their animal, they will have to pay patent royalties. This is not only absurd, it's macabre.

UNIT 8 *What's it all for?*

Excerpt from a radio interview involving an interviewer and two guest speakers.

Ronald Baker: ... Can we move on to the idea of effective education? Are our present institutions achieving this? .. Er, ..

Shirley James: Modern educational institutions can't be said to be faultless. Of course people will always moan about the curriculum. Others will find fault with teachers and school authorities, people will gripe over exams and complain about assessment and certainly, there's no point in denying that there are sometimes reasons to complain. We're really most concerned with the idea of improving the present system. And these improvements take time ...

Alan Fox: Well, of course people are going to complain ...

Shirley James: ... and sorry, if I could just finish. But we're investing more and more money in education .. erm .. in certain sectors of education, ones that most need improvement.

Alan Fox: Yes, you're talking about improving .. ah .. adjusting .. erm .. making minor adjustments to a system that's far from satisfactory. The type of system that you're supporting is .. well, elitist, it ... *

Shirley James: Surely, you must agree that the level of elitism of eh .. within our education system can only reflect what the public wants. The country voted for a government with certain educational ideas and the present system only reflects the will of the people ...

Alan Fox: Let's face it, most established systems contain certain elements of elitism ...

Ronald Baker: Yes, I'm sure we all agree, Mr. Fox, that traces of this elitism can be found everywhere, but you must admit that the type of education that you are advocating in your book is also elitist in a way .. in a different way perhaps, .. but ..

Alan Fox: Can I take you up on that? Erm, I'm not for a minute suggesting that all individuals should, or could indeed, take the steps the hero in my book does ...

Shirley James: Then surely you are writing about an elite minority, about people who feel that they have a choice, people that can give up modern living, people who feel they can pack in schooling as we know it and seek out a .. sort of back to nature .. er, return to the earth sort of existence. Surely that kind of move takes a courage and a knowledge of the world that we don't all possess.

Alan Fox: Let me stress that I have nowhere stated or suggested that this type of escape is the answer. In my book I pose it as an alternative, an extreme one perhaps. What I have said ...

Shirley James: But, Mr. Fox, you are advocating deschooling our society, to coin Illich's well worn phrase ...

Alan Fox: I'll come to that in a moment. If I may continue ... I have never said that my ideal society is without some form of education. I simply advocate a lesser dependence on present institutions. You see, I feel that more education could happen in the home and in the natural environment, away from ... outside the constricting school walls.

Shirley James: Let's not forget, Mr. Fox, that the revised curriculum also stresses the idea of continuous education and that implies taking education beyond the classroom while ...

Alan Fox: Mrs. James, what you are talking about is encouraging kids, and adults for that matter, to watch even more television than they do already, and I'm afraid that ...

Shirley James: With respect, your preoccupation with the Education through the Media Plan is a little exaggerated ...

Ronald Baker: Yes, this is all very interesting, very interesting indeed. But we've deviated rather from the original question. Can I remind you of the issues: is our present education system effective? ...

UNIT 2 *Teacher's script for test on page 41 of this book*

Section 1

Read these sentences aloud once. They should be spoken at conversational speed, not dictation speed. Pause for 5 seconds after each sentence.

1 The police are looking for a young, bald man with glasses and a beard.
2 He was wearing a short-sleeved checked shirt.
3 He is believed to have thrown a large five-sided coin with straight edges at the goalkeeper.
4 One of the other players said the suspect was standing to the right of the goalkeeper and immediately to the left of the right-hand goal post.
5 The incident provides further evidence of the rapid rise in football violence that has occurred this year after the slight decline shown in the previous two years.
6 There have been more convictions for robbery than murder and tax evasion together.
7 When he fell face down, the robber had a gun in his left hand, bank-notes in his right hand and was wearing shorts.
8 Which rectangle is divided into squares of equal size?
9 How long is the rectangle above a triangle which is next to a square?
10 Which set of shapes shows a triangle and rectangle in the middle with a square at each end?

Answers to Unit 2 test

Section 1		Section 2		Section 3	
1	*B*	11	*D*	19	*D*
2	*E*	12	*B*	20	*D*
3	*D*	13	*C*	21	*C*
4	*C*	14	*D*	22	*C*
5	*A*	15	*B*	23	*C*
6	*A*	16	*A*	24	*A*
7	*A*	17	*A*	25	*C*
8	*B*	18	*C*	26	*D*
9	*D*			27	*B*
10	*C*			28	*A*

Answers to Unit 3 test

Part 1		Part 2		Part 3		Part 4	
1	*D*	8	*B*	12	*B*	16	*A*
2	*B*	9	*D*	13	*C*	17	*B*
3	*D*	10	*A*	14	*A*	18	*D*
4	*A*	11	*D*	15	*D*	19	*A*
5	*C*						
6	*D*						
7	*A*						

Part 5		Part 6		Part 7		Part 8	
20	*D*	30	*B*	32	*A*	35	*C*
21	*D*	31	*A*	33	*C*	36	*A*
22	*A*			34	*D*	37	*C*
23	*C*						
24	*D*						
25	*B*						
26	*A*						
27	*B*						
28	*B*						
29	*C*						

General Questions	
38	*D*
39	*B*
40	*C*

Answers to Unit 4 test

1*a* This is a very complete table. Students may come up with something less complicated, but equally valid.

Table to show why arable land is under threat

Cause	Cause/Effect	Cause/Effect	Cause/Effect	Effect
Intensive farming	Salts ↗ Toxic chemicals ↗	Land degradation		
	Overgrazing Overcropping Salinisation Exposure of soil to wind and rain	Soil erosion	Desertification	Arable Land Under Threat
Lack of fuel	Burning of organic fertiliser	Loss of organic matter in topsoil		
Need for more land for building	Felling of rainforests	Deforestation		
Scarcity of timber		CO_2 ↗ + greenhouse effect ↗	Climatic change	
		Threat to genetic resources		

b One possible version of this flow chart could look like this:

Flow-chart to show development of Hawaii since 15th century

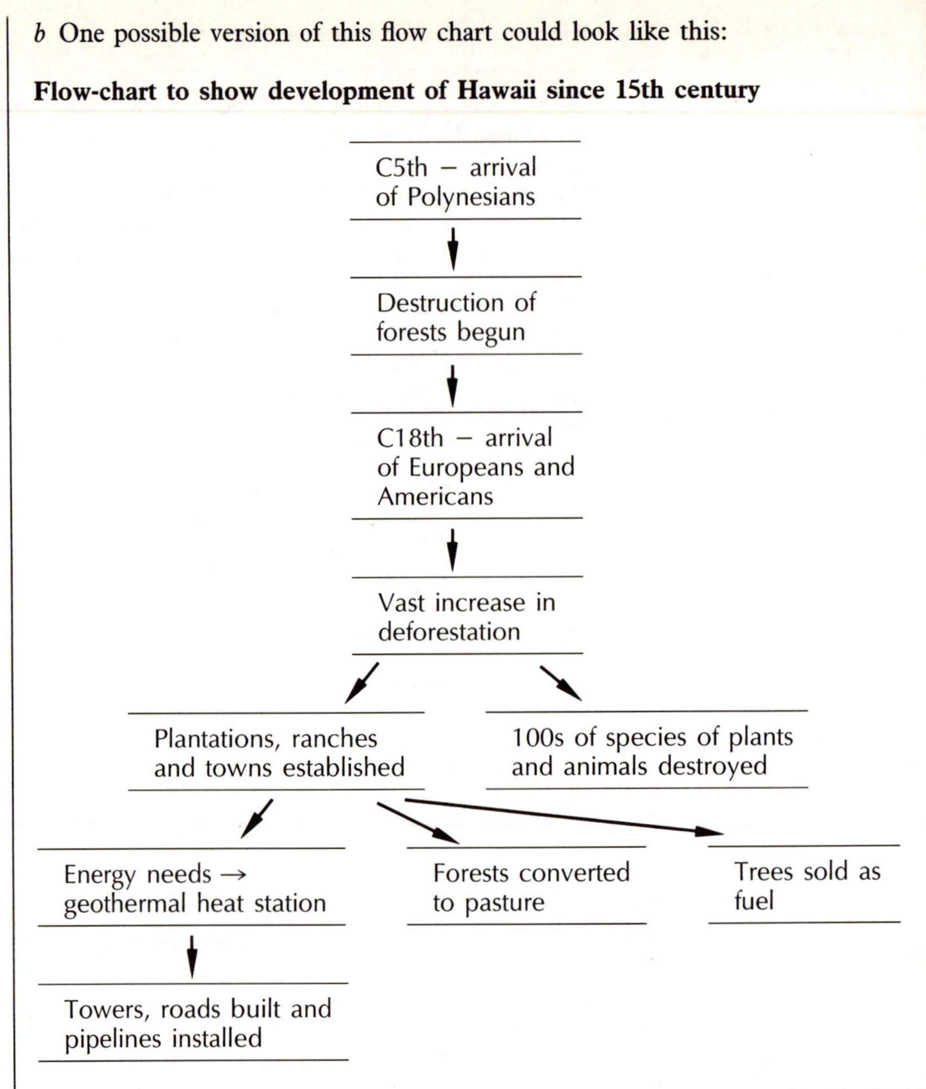

Answers to Unit 7 test

Section 1

1	*C*	**8**	*C*	**15**	*C*	**22**	*C*
2	*D*	**9**	*B*	**16**	*B*	**23**	*B*
3	*A*	**10**	*A*	**17**	*B*	**24**	*D*
4	*C*	**11**	*C*	**18**	*D*	**25**	*C*
5	*D*	**12**	*D*	**19**	*C*	**26**	*C*
6	*B*	**13**	*A*	**20**	*B*	**27**	*D*
7	*A*	**14**	*D*	**21**	*C*		

Section 2
Suggested answers

1 *a*

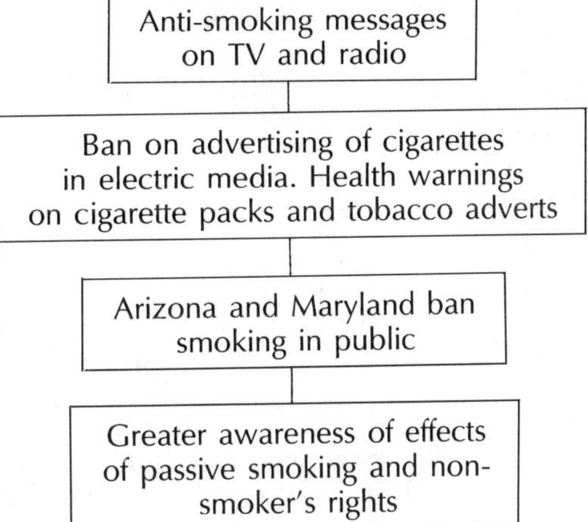

b The note-making for this talk is quite complicated as students must only record the anti-smoking policies which are beneficial to smokers as well.

Anti-smoking policies	Effects on smokers
Banning use of tobacco	Thousands of lives may be saved
Enforcing ban on public smoking	May encourage them to stop completely
Stigmatizing of smoking	Will make smoking socially unattractive
Tax increase	Reduced consumption

In marking the second question you should not be too concerned with the students' ideas themselves. You should pay special attention to the clarity with which they are expressed and the correctness of the grammar and structures used.

Answers to Unit 8 test

Part 1	Part 2	Part 3
1 *B*	9 *D*	15 *A*
2 *D*	10 *C*	16 *D*
3 *B*	11 *B*	17 *C*
4 *D*	12 *D*	18 *A*
5 *D*	13 *A*	
6 *A*	14 *C*	
7 *B*	15 *A*	
8 *B*	16 *D*	
General	**Part 4**	**Part 5**
19 *B*	22 *C*	24 *B*
20 *A*	23 *D*	25 *A*
21 *D*		

INTERVIEW

Below is a series of questions which could form the basis for a practice interview.

A selection of questions from each section could be asked in an interview. How many questions are asked from each section will depend on how quickly the answers come and how full the answers are.

The questions could be asked by the teacher in a one-to-one interview situation. They can also be read out by the teacher to the class in rapid succession, so that individual students are called on to answer, while the other students listen and assess.

Alternatively, the questions can be distributed to the students, who can then conduct mock interviews in groups or pairs.

A Personal questions

- Where do you come from?
- Tell me something about your hometown.
- Is there anything special about it?
- What do people there generally do for a living?
- Would you recommend your hometown to tourists?
- Do you come from a large family?
- Where do you come in the family?
- What do you imagine your family is doing at this moment?
- How do you spend your free time at home?
- If your sources were unlimited and you had as much free time as you wanted, what would you do?
- Have you read any good books lately – or seen any good films?
- What did you do during the last holidays?
- Tell me something about your present studies.
- What aspects of this educational establishment do you like/dislike?

B Text related questions

Note: All these questions relate to the texts in Unit 8.

- Which of the texts would you read if you were thinking of studying computing?
- What do you think the illustration on page 163 represents?
- In the text 'Growing Up With Computers' on page 164 we learn that people have different attitudes to computers.
  Which of the categories mentioned do you think you belong to? Why?
- The texts suggest that not being able to handle computers is a severe disadvantage these days. Do you agree?
- Which of the views on education described in the texts on pages 155–159 would you identify with most?
- What do you understand by the phrase 'Yuppie puppie'?
- Do you think that the advertisement on page 169 is an effective one? Why?

C Studies/career

- Where will you go from here?
- How do you see your future academic career?
- What do you imagine you will be doing in ten years time?
- What is your parents' attitude to your future plans?
- What factors influence you when you are making future plans?
- Why is English important to you?

NOTES

NOTES

NOTES

NOTES

NOTES

NOTES